Thorsten Meinl

Maximum-Score Diversity Selection

Thorsten Meinl

Maximum-Score Diversity Selection

A study on the selection of the best and most diverse

Südwestdeutscher Verlag für Hochschulschriften

Imprint
Any brand names and product names mentioned in this book are subject to trademark, brand or patent protection and are trademarks or registered trademarks of their respective holders. The use of brand names, product names, common names, trade names, product descriptions etc. even without a particular marking in this work is in no way to be construed to mean that such names may be regarded as unrestricted in respect of trademark and brand protection legislation and could thus be used by anyone.

Publisher:
Südwestdeutscher Verlag für Hochschulschriften
is a trademark of
Dodo Books Indian Ocean Ltd., member of the OmniScriptum S.R.L Publishing group
str. A.Russo 15, of. 61, Chisinau-2068, Republic of Moldova Europe
Printed at: see last page
ISBN: 978-3-8381-2009-6

Zugl. / Approved by: Konstanz, Universität, Diss., 2010

Copyright © Thorsten Meinl
Copyright © 2010 Dodo Books Indian Ocean Ltd., member of the OmniScriptum S.R.L Publishing group

Contents

1 **Introduction and Motivation**   1
    1.1 Structure of the thesis 4
    1.2 Notation 6

2 **MSDS in Early Drug Discovery**   7
    2.1 Distance measures for molecules 7
    2.2 Efficient MCSS computation 12
    2.3 Estimation of score values 16

3 **Formalization of Maximum-Score Diversity Selection**   21
    3.1 Measures for diversity 21
    3.2 Maximum-score diversity selection is $\mathcal{NP}$-hard 30

4 **Multi-objective Optimization**   35
    4.1 General optimization 35
    4.2 Linear optimization 36
    4.3 Combinatorial optimization 39
    4.4 Multiple objectives 42
        4.4.1 The dominance relation 43
        4.4.2 Ranking Pareto front approximations by indicator functions 45
        4.4.3 Solving multi-objective optimization problems 47
    4.5 Turning MSDS into a single-objective problem 50

5 **Metaheuristics for Optimization Problems**   53
    5.1 Single-objective genetic algorithms 55
    5.2 Multi-objective genetic algorithms 57
    5.3 Genetic representations and operators for subsets 62
        5.3.1 Binary subset genomes and SX-crossover 64
        5.3.2 Integer subset genomes with two-point crossover 64
        5.3.3 Integer subset genomes with uniform crossover 65

		5.3.4 Permutation-based subsets	66

6	**Heuristic Approaches**		**69**
	6.1	Erkut's p-dispersion heuristic	69
	6.2	Hochbaum & Shmoys' p-center heuristic	70
	6.3	Score Erosion	72

7	**Experimental Evaluation on Artificial Data**		**75**
	7.1	Influence of genetic representations and operators	76
	7.2	Deficiencies of the genetic algorithm	78
	7.3	Results with different heuristics	79
		7.3.1 Pareto front approximations	81
		7.3.2 Runtimes	83
	7.4	Influence of the search space structure	85
		7.4.1 Influence of peak count on solution quality	85
		7.4.2 Behavior of the diversity functions	85

8	**Experiments and Applications on Molecular Datasets**		**93**
	8.1	MSDS on molecules	93
		8.1.1 Influence of genetic representations and operators	94
		8.1.2 Pareto front approximations	97
		8.1.3 Practical results	102
	8.2	MSDS for feature selection	104

9	**Conclusions**	**107**

A	**Complexity Theoretic Preliminaries**	**111**

Chapter 1

Introduction and Motivation

Selection is a process that each human performs many times a day. Be it at the cafeteria when it comes to choosing main and side-dishes for lunch, at the car dealer when it comes to choosing which extras are worth their price and which are not, or when you have to decide who of your numerous friends gets a card for Christmas and who not. All these choices of a certain number of objects from a bigger set of available objects are based on one or more criteria. However, quite naturally for humans, it is hard to actually define these criteria and the chosen subset is more a matter of intuition than of a sound optimization of all criteria. For such everyday selections this approach may be acceptable, but there are other similar situations where selecting the right subset is crucial.

A common subset selection problem arises during the development of new drugs in pharmaceutical companies. The path that that starts with a disease and ends in a drug that cures it is extremely long (> 10 years) and costs a lot of money [28]. Figure 1.1 shows a graphical depiction of the so-called *pipeline* that characterizes the development of new drugs.

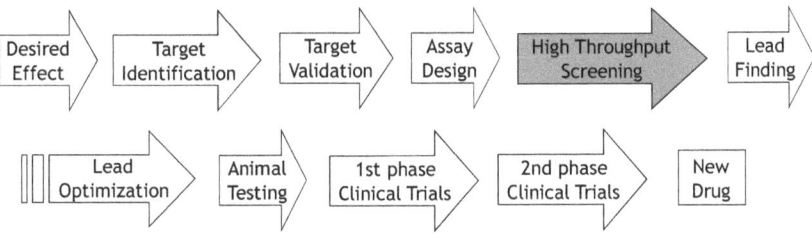

Figure 1.1: The drug development pipeline.

After the desired effect (e.g. a drug against lung cancer) has been chosen, the "target" inside the human body has to be identified. Usually this is a protein, whose behavior is, in some sense peculiar (e.g. because it is produced too often). Next, a set of simple hand-made experiments are performed in order to validate that the chosen target is in fact the right one. The following step is the so-called assay design in which a simple, fast, and cheap test must be found with which several hundreds of thousand of molecules can be tested automatically.

Contrary to what a lot of people assume, in its early stages, drug design entails nothing more than looking for the proverbial needle in a haystack, and is known as *High Throughput Screening* (HTS) in this context [65]. Every pharmaceutical company has a large library of molecules (up to millions) that they repeatedly use for each new project in order to find some so-called *hits*. These are molecules that show the desired reaction in the used assay. Only after a number of promising molecules has been identified during lead finding are they further optimized in the lead optimization phase. This comprises many iterations of experiments, structural modifications, and computer-aided simulations. Once one (or in rare cases some) drug candidate has been found it is first tested in animals and then enters the clinical trials stages. If everything runs successfully during these 10 to 12 years of research, at the end, a new drug will have been found and can be sold.

During the research period, selections have to be made at many stages. One particularly interesting selection is usually required right before HTS starts. Companies' libraries are always growing, as before the start of HTS, a small collection of new molecules is bought specifically for the respective project. The important question is: how are these few thousand molecules selected from a set of the several million that can be bought from numerous vendors? Of course the selection could be purely random, but the chance that any of the selected molecules turns out to be biologically active (i.e. it shows the desired effect) afterwards is rather small. This is when *virtual High Throughput Screening* (vHTS) comes into play [5]. There are several methods, some of which are described later on in Section 2.3, that can predict the activity of molecules. Of course there is no method that is perfect and chemists are not persuaded of virtual methods – the main reason why real HTS is still performed. But they can at least be used to rank molecules and reduce a set of several millions to some thousands, which are subsequently purchased and tested in the following HTS. Thus, one criteria for the optimal selection of a subset is quite easy to define: select molecules whose (predicted) activity is as high as possible. In the context of vHTS methods the term activity is usually replaced by *score* since the computed numerical values do not have anything to do with real activity values (with the exception that high score values should be somehow related to high activity values afterwards). This is the origin of the first part of the title of this thesis: *maximum-score*.

Unfortunately, matters are not that simple: one fundamental principle in drug discovery is the *structure-activity relationship* (SAR), which states that similar molecules (=similar structure) demonstrate similar biological activity. As a consequence the probability of the selection, for example, of the 1,000 highest-ranking molecules, after vHTS, yielding a large group of similar molecules is quite high. In principle there could also be many diverse molecules with equally high activities but in practice this is rarely observed. This poses a problem for various reasons: first, if one common substructure of these similar molecules turns out to be covered by a competitor's patent the whole group containing this fragment is essentially rendered useless. The same happens if a substructure causes negative side-effects. Second, lead finding and optimization need many structurally different hits from HTS, because if the only active group (containing similar hits) cannot be optimized for any reason the project will die and have wasted a lot of money and time. Therefore, the more distinct starting points are available for lead optimization the better. This results in the second criteria for selecting which suitable subset of molecules should be bought: the molecules in the selected subset should be (structurally) as diverse as possible. This makes up the second part of the title: *diversity*.

These tasks have been dealt with to a certain extent in the chemoinformatics community, and yet, to the best of our knowledge, to date no one has taken both into account at the same time. Combining both criteria leads to the *maximum-score diversity selection* (MSDS) problem. As already indicated, optimizing both criteria at the same time may pose a problem because structural diversity and activity are conflicting objectives.

Similar problems also arise in other application areas. In economics, portfolio selection [47] has also (at least) two different goals: on the one hand, selected stocks should perform well, i.e. have a high "score", and on the other, the portfolio should be diverse so that a retracement in one segment of the market does not affect all stocks in the portfolio but only a few. This is clearly another instance of maximum-score diversity selection. However, how stock scores (rating, performance over last x months, ...) and the diversity of a set of stocks (industrial sectors, price dependencies over time, ...) are measured is not as obvious as for molecules.

Another more abstract application of MSDS is in the field of frequent or discriminative pattern mining, which tries to find re-occurring patterns in a huge set of objects (see [32] for an overview). Common examples are itemsets, e.g. customer transactions in supermarkets, where subsets of items that are often bought together are of interest, or graphs, e.g. the 2D structure of molecules, where frequent subgraphs may explain the behavior of certain molecules in (bio)chemical reactions. One drawback of most approaches is that the number of discovered patterns is much too large to be useful. Often more patterns are found than objects. One way to sensibly reduce the amount is to select the most frequent (i.e. with a high score) *and* diverse patterns enabling the whole pattern space to be covered. This can be interpreted as a kind of feature selection.

Regardless of the specific application area, MSDS can always be formulated in the same way. A subset S with p objects is to be selected such that the following two objectives are optimized at the same time:

$$\text{Maximize } f_1(S) = \sum_{u \in S} \sigma(u) \tag{1.1}$$

$$\text{Maximize } f_2(S) = \delta(S) \tag{1.2}$$

where $|S| = p$, σ returns the score of an object, and δ is any reasonable diversity function. These are the two important functions around which this thesis is built. Several questions arise from these two objectives:

1. How are subset scores measured? This tends to be a simpler sub-problem to solve since the score is an independent property of each single object.

2. How is the diversity of a selected subset determined? This question is much more com-

plicated, because diversity is a property of the whole subset and is usually derived from a pairwise relation between the objects such as a distance or similarity measure.

3. Given that both the score and the diversity of a subset can be computed, what does an optimal subset look like and how is it found?

Therefore the goals of this thesis are as follows: First, since the original motivation was the selection of molecules for usage in HTS, we discuss how the two main prerequisites for MSDS – scores for the molecules and a sensible distance measure from which diversity is derived – are best computed for molecules. Computing the distance between two molecules is a particularly complex problem, for which a comparably fast algorithm is presented.

The second goal is to find a suitable definition of diversity that is not only intuitive and formally sound but also easy to compute. We discover that there are quite a few existing definitions for diversity but most of them are either not suitable for the general case of MSDS, too time-consuming to compute, or result in undesirable distributions of objects in the selected subset.

The third objective is to find one or more algorithms that efficiently find subsets that optimize both criteria, score and diversity. We show that MSDS is an $\mathcal{NP}$-hard problem that cannot be solved efficiently. Therefore heuristic algorithms are the only way to solve common instances of MSDS. In fact, MSDS is a typical hard *multi-objective optimization problem*, for which general algorithms exist. However, we demonstrate that these existing general algorithms are either not applicable, too slow, or produce incomplete and inferior results compared to other algorithms. With respect to the latter two issues, (partial) solutions are developed. Since the results continue to disappoint, several other heuristic approaches are presented involving modifications of existing single-objective algorithms. Additionally we propose a novel algorithm that is faster than all existing approaches.

The fourth aim involves performing an extensive set of experiments that supports the conclusions made about the behavior, solution and runtime of the presented algorithms.

1.1 Structure of the thesis

This thesis is structured as follows: The second chapter considers the application of MSDS in chemoinformatics. We discuss several practical issues in this context, such as computing scores for molecules that correlate with their real activities, and efficient distance computation between molecules. Since one crucial aspect of MSDS is the diversity criteria, Chapter 3 discusses various possibilities possibilities of defining diversity and their pros and cons. In this chapter we also show that MSDS is an $\mathcal{NP}$-hard optimization problem justifying the usage of heuristic approaches. We have already mentioned that MSDS is a multi-objective optimization problem. Therefore Chapter 4 introduces the concepts of general optimization, linear optimization, combinatorial optimization, and finally multi-objective optimization. Especially the latter requires sophisticated methods of determining the quality of solutions when compared to single-objective problems. The chapter concludes with a description of state-of-the-art approaches to solve multi-objective optimization problems.

Judging from the vast amount of publications probably the most popular approach to solving multi-objective optimization problems is metaheuristics, most notably genetic algorithms. We begin Chapter 5 describing the general ideas of genetic algorithms. One main aspect is the right choice of the so-called genetic representation and the corresponding operators. Since MSDS is a subset selection problem we discuss representations and operators for optimizing subsets of objects in more detail, including a set of novel operators. Finally, we explain the necessary modifications of genetic algorithms for multiple objectives and present three popular multi-objective genetic algorithms.

Chapter 6 describes two well-known heuristics for selecting diverse subsets and how they can be applied to MSDS. Since both algorithms are rather slow on large numbers of objects, we present the novel *Score Erosion Algorithm*, which runs much faster.

All presented algorithms are extensively evaluated in Chapters 7 and 8. In the former synthetic datasets are used in order to compare the various genetic operators discussed in Chapter 5, and all heuristics. Also the influence of the search space structure and the chosen diversity measure is discussed. In the latter chapter a similar set of experiments is performed on real-world molecular datasets. Their purpose is to check if the results on synthetic data are transferable and also to check if MSDS is useful in practice. The chapter concludes with a demonstration of how MSDS can be used effectively in a feature selection scenario. The results of this thesis are summed up in Chapter 9.

1.2 Notation

The following notations are used throughout the whole thesis. Additional symbols, which are only relevant for certain parts are introduced as they occur.

Symbol	Meaning
I	Set of all objects under consideration
S	Set of selected objects; a subset of I
u, v	Elements from S (or I, depending on the context)
p	Number of selected objects; $|S| = p$
$\sigma(\cdot)$	Function that assigns a score to each object; all scores are assumed to be normalized between 0 and 1
$d(\cdot, \cdot)$	Function that returns distance between two objects; all distances are assumed to be normalized between 0 and 1
$\delta(\cdot)$	Function that computes a (sub)set's diversity
α	Weighting parameter to express preferences between two objectives
β	Weighting parameter used in Score Erosion

Chapter 2

MSDS in Early Drug Discovery

Although MSDS can be applied in a number of areas, the most prominent domain and the initial motivation for this thesis is its application in early drug discovery. Therefore in this chapter both parts of MSDS in the context of molecules are discussed more thoroughly. First, distance measures for molecules are presented (from which later on the diversity of a set of molecules is derived). Second, we discuss an intuitive measure, which suits the task of MSDS well and is based on the size of the maximum common substructure between two molecules. As the computation of this measure is complex, we show an efficient way of computing it. To conclude this chapter, a short overview on estimating molecule activity is provided.

2.1 Distance measures for molecules

One of the key issues in chemoinformatics is the concept of molecular similarity. There are dozens (if not hundreds) of publications about general aspects of similarity and specific algorithms. Good and broad overviews can be found in [7] or [44]. Therefore the following is only a short summary of the three different groups of similarity measures.

The first group are the so-called fingerprints, which are bit-strings of fixed length. Each bit encodes the presence or absence of a specific feature in the molecule under consideration, e.g. existence of hydrogen donors or acceptors, of carbonyl groups, etc. The number of features can easily reach more than a thousand and each vendor has its own collection. The similarity between two fingerprints is usually determined with the Tanimoto coefficient between the two binary vectors $\boldsymbol{x}$ and $\boldsymbol{y}$:

$$s_{Tan}(\boldsymbol{x}, \boldsymbol{y}) = \frac{\sum_{i=1}^{n} x_i y_i}{\sum_{i=1}^{n}(x_i + y_i - x_i y_i)} \qquad (2.1)$$

The nominator is the sum of bits (i.e. features) that are present in both molecules, whereas the denominator is the total sum of features in both molecules minus the common features. Since the Tanimoto coefficient takes on values between zero and one it can easily be converted into a distance by taking one minus the coefficient. The big advantage of fingerprints is that they can be computed very easily and fast and their performance when it comes to building predictive models is surprisingly good. However, they are still an abstraction of the real molecule and lack important structural information. In principle it is possible to also encode structural information in fingerprints, e.g. by defining features such as "a nitrogen atom within three bonds distance of an oxygen atom". However, this would blow up their size dramatically, because each bit position has a fixed meaning for all molecules and all possible combinations would have to be encoded. Additionally, modeling the quantity of a feature (e.g. number of hydrogen donors or the solvent accessible surface area) is also cumbersome.

Hence, the second group is formed by a vast amount of numeric descriptors, such as surface area, molecular weight, or simply the number of features. A sensible collection of these descriptors is then combined into a feature vector and usually the Euclidean distance is used to compute the similarity between two vectors. One problem with this approach is the different scales of properties: whereas the molecular weight is commonly measured in atomic units ranging between 200 and 800 for drug-like compounds, the number of hydrogen donors/or acceptors is mostly below 10. One possible solution is to work with normalized values, but the normalization factors are then dependent on the actual data and may be inappropriate for yet unseen molecules. Similar to fingerprints, the numeric descriptors are efficiently computable but are still a high-level abstraction of a molecule.

The third group of approaches operates more or less directly on the molecules by using their 2D or 3D structure. Unfortunately, most of these graph-based approaches suffer from the lack of efficient algorithms because they usually involve the computation of common subgraphs, which is an $\mathcal{NP}$-hard problem (at least for general graphs). Three-dimensional approaches are affected by alignment problems, which is a research area of its own. Consequently, most structure-based similarity measures still use some kind of abstraction. A very popular tool are the so-called *Feature Trees* [60]. Here the functional parts of molecules (e.g. aromatic rings, hydrogenous donors/acceptors) are represented as nodes in the tree, whose structure resembles the original molecular structure. The restriction to trees enables the usage of efficient matching algorithms for comparing them and computing a similarity. Another structure-based approach is Cofea, the compressed feature matrix [2]. Similar to Feature Trees, functional parts in the molecules are identified and their pairwise distances in the molecule are encoded in a matrix. The similarity is then based on the occurrences of similar patterns in the compressed feature matrices. Locating them is similar to the subgraph isomorphism problem (see below), but since the feature matrices are smaller than the original molecular graphs the algorithm is still reasonably fast.

Besides the above-mentioned, structure-based similarity measures, which work on abstractions of the molecular graph, we decided to work directly on the graphs. This was particularly appropriate since the definition of clusters, which are starting points for further lead optimization, is usually based on the structures and not abstractions thereof.

However before we introduce our graph-based distance measure, we first need to define some graph terminology.

Definition 1. *A graph $G = (V, E)$ consists of two sets V and E, the former containing the graphs' nodes or vertices and the latter containing its edges. An edge is a tuple of nodes*

$\{x, y\}$ (for undirected graphs). A labeled graph $G = (V, E, l_V, l_E)$ additionally has two functions $l_V : V \to L_V$ and $l_E : E \to L_E$ that assign arbitrary labels (numbers, names) to all nodes and edges, respectively. The degree of a node x is the number of other nodes it is connected to via an edge: $deg(x) = |\{y | \{x, y\} \in E\}|$.

For molecules the nodes' labels are usually the element numbers and the edges' labels are the bond types (single, double, triple, or aromatic).

Definition 2. *A graph is* connected *if there is a sequence of edges* $(\{x_1, x_2\}, ..., \{x_{k-1}, x_k\})$, $x_i \in V, x_1 \neq x_k$ *with* $\{x_i, x_{i+1}\} \in E, i = 1, ..., k$ *between all pairs of nodes. Otherwise the graph consists of several* connected components, *each of which is itself connected.*

A common task is to check whether two graphs are identical. This is done by finding a so-called graph isomorphism.

Definition 3. *A function* $f : V_1 \to V_2$ *is called a* graph isomorphism *between two graphs G_1 and G_2 if*

- *f is bijective*

- $l_1(x) = l_2(f(x))$, *i.e. corresponding nodes have the same label*

- $\{x, y\} \in E_1$ *if and only if* $\{f(x), f(y)\} \in E_2$, *i.e. if there is an edge between x and y in G_1 then there is also an edge between the mapped nodes $f(x)$ and $f(y)$, or there is no such edge in both graphs*

- $l_1(\{x, y\}) = l_2(\{f(x), f(y)\})$, *i.e. corresponding edges have equal labels*

If such a function f exists, then G_1 and G_2 are isomorphic or, to put it more simply, equal. The question as to whether or not two graphs are isomorphic is a problem in $\mathcal{NP}$ but it is still unclear if it is $\mathcal{NP}$-complete (it is supposed to be in the gap between $\mathcal{P}$ and $\mathcal{NP}$-complete). Currently no polynomial time algorithm is known, except for special graph classes, such as bounded-degree or planar graphs.

Similar to the problem of the equality of two graphs is the question of whether or not one graph is part of another graph, or if a subgraph isomorphism exists between the two graphs.

Definition 4. *A graph $G_1 = (V_1, E_1, l_V, l_E)$ is called a* subgraph *of $G_2 = (V_2, E_2, l_V, l_E)$ if $V_1 \subseteq V_2$ and $E_1 \subseteq E_2$. A function $f : V_1 \to V_2$ is called a* subgraph isomorphism, *if*

- *f in injective*

- $l_1(x) = l_2(f(x))$, *i.e. corresponding nodes have the same label*

- $\{x, y\} \in E_1$ *if $\{f(x), f(y)\} \in E_2$, i.e. if there is an edge between x and y in G_1 then there is also an edge between the mapped nodes $f(x)$ and $f(y)$ (but not necessarily the other way round)*

- $l_1(\{x,y\}) = l_2(\{f(x), f(y)\})$, i.e. *corresponding edges have equal labels*

The subgraph isomorphism problem, i.e. deciding if G_1 is an (induced) subgraph of G_2, is $\mathcal{NP}$-complete [27].

One possible way of defining structural similarity between a pair of molecules is to look at the *maximum common substructure* (MCSS, also known as maximum common subgraph). The MCSS is a well-known and established concept in chemoinformatics and many algorithms are based on it. An example for the MCSS between two molecules is shown in Figure 2.1. Speaking in graph-theoretic terms, the MCSS of G_1 and G_2 is the biggest, usually connected, graph that is both a subgraph of G_1 and G_2 (an exact definition of MCSS and its specific types is given in Section 2.2). The size of the MCSS of two molecules can be used to construct a similarity,

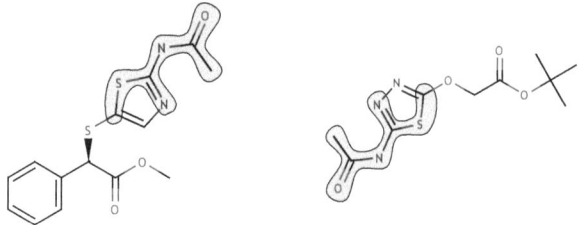

Figure 2.1: Maximum common substructure of two molecules.

which in turn can easily be extended to a distance measure on molecules or, in general, graphs.

Definition 5. *The MCSS-based similarity measure is defined as* $s_{mcss}(A,B) = \frac{|mcss(A,B)|^2}{|A|*|B|}$. *Likewise we define the corresponding distance measure as* $d_{mcss}(A,B) = 1 - s_{mcss}(A,B)$.

That is, the similarity between two molecules is the square of the size of the maximum common substructure divided by the product of the sizes of both molecules. The size of a molecule (and hence also the MCSS) can be measured as the number of atoms, edges or even better their sum. Since the size of the MCSS can be at most as large as the smaller of the two molecules, s_{mcss} is always between 0 and 1. Consequently the distance d_{mcss} is also in the same range. One interesting question is whether this definition satisfies the mathematical conditions for a metric.

Definition 6. *A function $m(x,y)$ is called a* metric *if it satisfies the following constraints:*

- $m(x,x) = 0$, i.e. *objects have a distance of 0 to themselves*
- $m(x,y) = 0 \Rightarrow x = y$, i.e. *if two objects have zero distance then they are equal*
- $m(x,y) = m(y,x)$, i.e. *the distance function is symmetric*
- $m(x,y) \leq m(x,z) + m(z,y)$, i.e. *the triangle inequality is satisfied*

Theorem 1. *The MCSS-based distance measure* $d_{mcss}(A,B) = 1 - \frac{|mcss(A,B)|^2}{|A|*|B|}$ *is a metric.*

Proof. The first property is trivially satisfied, because the MCSS between a molecule and itself is the molecule and thus both nominator and denominator are equal. The second property is also true in all cases, because for the distance to be zero it must hold that $|A|*|B| = |mcss(A,B)|^2$. As we have already seen $|mcss(A,B)| \leq min(|A|,|B|)$ and thus $|A|*|B| \leq min(|A|,|B|)^2$. This can only be true if A and B have the same size. Additionally, the size of their MCSS can only be the same as both A and B if it is isomorphic to both A *and* B. Consequently A and B must also be isomorphic to each other, which means they represent the same object. The third property is again trivially true, since the MCSS does not depend on the order of the two graphs.

Property four is a bit more complicated to prove. There are two cases to distinguish:

- $d_{mcss}(x,z) \geq d_{mcss}(x,y)$ or $d_{mcss}(z,y) \geq d_{mcss}(x,y)$
- $d_{mcss}(x,z) < d_{mcss}(x,y)$ and $d_{mcss}(z,y) < d_{mcss}(x,y)$

In the first case, it is easy to see that the triangle inequality is always satisfied, thus the interesting case is the second. Both inequalities can be transformed to

$$s_{mcss}(x,z) > s_{mcss}(x,y) \tag{2.2}$$
$$s_{mcss}(z,y) > s_{mcss}(x,y) \tag{2.3}$$

The triangle inequality can be simplified to

$$s_{mcss}(x,z) + s_{mcss}(z,y) - 1 \leq s_{mcss}(x,y) \tag{2.4}$$

Replacing the right-hand side with one of the inequalities 2.2 or 2.3 yields

$$s_{mcss}(x,z) + s_{mcss}(z,y) - 1 \leq s_{mcss}(x,z) \tag{2.5}$$
$$s_{mcss}(z,y) \leq 1 \tag{2.6}$$

which follows from the definition of s_{mcss}. □

To conclude, d_{mcss} satisfies all conditions for a metric and thus certain algorithms, which rely on the distances being metric, (such as the one presented in Section 6.2) can be applied.

Coming back to the MCSS as a measure for molecular similarity, one drawback of the above strict definition is that so far it uses only the one maximum common connected substructure of two molecules. However, two molecules can frequently consist of two identical parts that are connected by a small bridge, which is different in both molecules. The MCSS is the bigger of the two parts and the smaller one is completely ignored. Therefore the two molecules have a low level of similarity even though they are identical but for maybe one single atom that forms the bridge, see Figure 2.2. A much better way of expressing the similarity is to take all *maximal common substructures*. A maximal common substructure is a subgraph of both G_1 and G_2 that cannot be extended any further (but it need not necessarily be the biggest of all such common

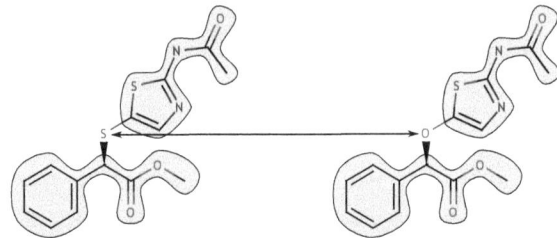

Figure 2.2: A pair of molecules with two maximal common substructures.

subgraphs). Re-defining the *mcss*-function so that it computes the set of all (non-overlapping) maximal common substructures results in a better and more intuitive sense of similarity. It still satisfies the only important property of *mcss* which is that it always returns a graph (now consisting of several unconnected components) that is at most as big as the smaller of both graphs G_1 and G_2.

2.2 Efficient MCSS computation

Speaking of "the" MCSS between two graphs is, in fact, not quite correct as there are various types of MCSS. Usually MCSS is categorized into *connected* and *induced* (or combinations thereof). A general MCSS is defined as the maximum graph H that is both a subgraph of G_1 and G_2. It may consist of several unconnected components. A connected MCSS consists of a single *connected component* only. One speaks of an induced MCSS if induced subgraph isomorphisms between the MCSS and both graphs exist.

Definition 7. *A function f is an* induced subgraph isomorphisms *if it is a subgraph isomorphism and*

- $\{x,y\} \in E_1$ *if and only if* $\{f(x), f(y)\} \in E_2$, *i.e. if there is an edge between x and y in G_1 then there is also an edge between the mapped nodes $f(x)$ and $f(y)$, or there is no edge in both graphs*

If H consists of only one connected component then it is the maximum common connected substructure (MCCSS). Figure 2.3 shows the difference between the MCSS, which consists of the gray and the yellow parts of the two molecules, and the MCCSS, which comprises the gray parts only. If H is an induced subgraph it is known as the maximum common induced substructure (MCISS). This is depicted in Figure 2.4. The general MCSS would also cover the two non-marked carbon atoms in both molecules, whereas the MCISS does not contain them. This is because the connection between the leftmost and rightmost carbon atom is missing in the right molecule and present in the left molecule, closing the ring. If H is both connected and induced it is called the maximum common connected induced subgraph (MCCISS). For molecules usually only MCCSS or or MCSS consisting of several large, connected components

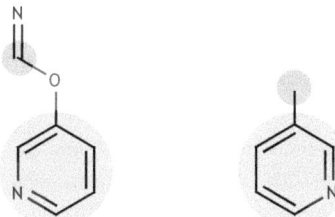

Figure 2.3: The figure shows the two molecules' connected (gray) and unconnected MCSS (gray and yellow).

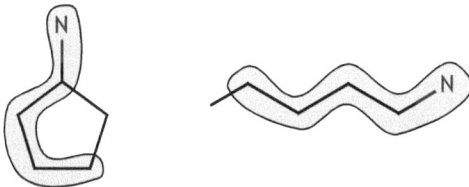

Figure 2.4: The figure shows the two molecules' maximum common *induced* substructure.

are of interest. Single atoms, which are mapped more or less arbitrarily, do not make any chemical or biological sense. The question, whether or not MCSS should be induced, depends on the specific application, however the latter tends to be used more often. They are also called maximum common connected *edge* subgraphs since a maximum matching of edges instead of nodes is sought.

Although induced and/or connected MCSS are restrictions to general MCSS their computation remains $\mathcal{NP}$-hard in all cases (except for special graph classes) [27]. This may be one reason why the MCSS is still seldom used as a similarity or distance measure between two molecules. Nevertheless a lot of algorithms have been invented for the MCSS problem, which can be categorized into three groups:

- Direct branch-and-bound approaches
- Maximum clique-based algorithms
- Heuristic approaches

Since molecules are rather small graphs there is usually no need to resort to heuristics, therefore we shall not discuss them any further. The first group is the most natural way of attacking the problem, and many algorithms exist (e.g. [3, 17, 40, 67]). The rough idea is to build a subgraph step by step that occurs in both G_1 and G_2. However, many of those compute general MCSS ([67, 40]) which is not only unsuitable for molecules but also considerably slower than the search for connected MCSS. Computing a connected MCSS between typical drug-like molecules, consisting of about 70 atoms, takes less than a second, whereas the general MCSS needs several minutes (using the algorithm from [40])!

The second group initially builds a so-called *compatibility* or *product* graph P, in which each node represents a pair of nodes (u, v) with $u \in V_{G_1}$, $v \in V_{G_2}$, and $l_{V_{G_1}}(u) = l_{V_{G_2}}(v)$. Thus, each node in P corresponds to a potential mapping of nodes from G_1 and G_2. Next, edges are added between two nodes $(u_1, v_1), (u_2, v_2) \in V_P$ if there are edges $\{u_1, u_2\} \in E_{G_1}$ and $\{v_1, v_2\} \in E_{G_2}$ (having the same label), or there are no edges in both graphs. This means that the mapping $u_1 \Leftrightarrow v_1$ and $u_2 \Leftrightarrow v_2$ is compatible. A *clique* in P then corresponds to a set of node-tuples from G_1 and G_2 that are pairwise compatible.

Definition 8. *A clique is a subset of nodes $V' \subseteq V$ such that $\forall x, y \in V', x \neq y : \{x, y\} \in E$, i.e. there is an edge between all pairs of nodes in V'.*

Deciding whether a graph contains a clique of size p, or greater, is an $\mathcal{NP}$-complete problem [27].

The node tuples in the clique form a common subgraph (not necessarily connected) in both G_1 and G_2. Consequently the *maximum* clique in P is an MCSS of G_1 and G_2. Due to this reduction from MCSS to MAXCLIQUE algorithms for the latter can be used to find MCSS. Most current algorithms are based on the Bron-Kerbosch algorithm [14]. For computing connected MCSS several modifications are necessary, but provide the added bonus that the search is performed much faster [39].

Which of the two approaches is faster depends considerably on the structure of the graph. For molecules, however, additional constraints may be of interest, such as the fact that rings should not be broken up, or that slight structural variations do not change chemical behavior (e.g. carbon and nitrogen atoms in rings can often be exchanged with each other). It would require major changes to existing MCSS algorithms to include these constraints, therefore we have chosen a different approach to compute the MCSS – and in fact *all* maximal common connected subgraphs – between two molecules. Although frequent subgraph mining (FSM) algorithms are usually used for more complex tasks they can also be applied to compute MCSS. Their main application is to find subgraphs that occur in at least a certain number of graphs in a graph database. The motivation behind FSM is to find interesting patterns in the data that can e.g. explain why a set of molecules is active or not. The MCSS problem is a special case of FSM where the database consists of only two graphs and the minimum support (i.e. the number of graphs in which the subgraph must occur) is set to 100%. It might seem surprising, but for molecules these algorithms seem to perform extraordinarily well in computing the MCSS even though they accomplish a more general task.

Frequent subgraph mining became an important research topic in the data mining community around the year 2000. Most algorithms were published in the years thereafter, including gSpan [70], FFSM [35], MoFa/MoSS [11] and Gaston [54]. The latter was the last milestone algorithm in FSM, since then only slight improvements on restricted kinds of graphs have been reported. One of the fastest algorithms is MoSS (formerly named MoFa). Since its invention in 2002 several improvements have been made, some of which are especially useful for MCSS computation in molecules.

Similar to branch-and-bound algorithms for MCSS the frequent subgraphs are built step-by-step. The search is started at nodes with the least common label. Then in all graphs all possible extensions with one edge and an atom are gathered and grouped. All these groups are potential extensions of the frequent subgraphs (or MCSS), but not all of them need to be performed. Extensions that occur in too few graphs can simply be discarded since the resulting subgraph (and all further subgraphs derived from it) is infrequent. This step is called *support based pruning*. In the case of MCSS the extension must be present in both graphs. Figure 2.5 shows an example with two graphs. Assuming the search is started with S, possible extensions are S-C and S-O. Whereas the former is possible in both graphs, the latter only occurs in the right graph and can therefore be discarded.

Figure 2.5: Two example molecules, the MCSS is built starting from the sulfur atom.

The second important step is *structural pruning*. Let us assume that the common substructure has grown to S-C. Now either =O or -N can be added. It is easy to see that in the end both are part of the MCSS, but a naive algorithm would try all possible combinations of adding the two extensions, i.e. first =O and then -N and the other way round. This is of course unnecessary work, therefore several sophisticated pruning rules are applied to try to avoid it. Current state-of-the-art algorithms rely on canonical codes for graphs, which represent the graph uniquely [10]. While the MCSS is grown step by step, the code is built according to the added edges and nodes. If at some point the subgraph's code does not resemble its canonical code, this branch of the search tree can be pruned. However, computing the canonical code (or checking if it is canonical or not) presents difficulties because it essentially solves the graph isomorphism problem (if two graphs have equal canonical codes they are isomorphic). Therefore MoSS additionally uses several simple rules in order to check if the search tree can be pruned. One such pruning type is *perfect extension pruning* [12]. It is motivated by the search for so-called *closed frequent subgraphs*. A subgraph is closed if there is no supergraph that occurs in the same number of graphs, i.e. it cannot be grown further without losing support in at least one graph. It is easy to see that the MCSS is a closed subgraph and hence the optimizations for closed subgraph mining can be applied.

Perfect extension pruning is based on the observation that sometimes there is a fairly large common fragment in all currently considered molecules (that is, in all molecules considered in a given branch of the search tree). From the definition of a closed fragment it is clear that in such a situation, if the current fragment is only a part of the common substructure, then any extension that does not grow the current fragment towards the maximal common one can be postponed until this maximal common fragment has been reached. That is, as long as the search has not grown a fragment to the maximal common one, it is not necessary to branch in the search tree. The reason is, obviously, that the maximal common fragment is part of all closed fragments that can be found in the currently considered set of molecules. Consequently, it suffices to follow only one path in the search tree that leads to this maximal common fragment and to first start branching at this point. The search for the MCSS is finished at this step, as any further extension will have already been discarded by support-based pruning. More details, potential pitfalls and how perfect extension pruning can be combined with canonical codes can be found in the above-mentioned article.

Another extension to MoSS that is useful for mining in molecules are so-called *ring extensions* [33]. Rings are treated as single entities and all their atoms and bonds are added to the growing subgraph in one step. This not only accelerates the search considerably, but also prevents open rings in frequent substructures or the MCSS. If in the example in Figure 2.4 ring extensions had been enabled, MCSS would consist of the nitrogen atom only, since all carbon atoms are part of a ring in the left molecules but not in the right. Dealing with complete rings is markedly more appropriate than allowing matches of ring/non-ring atoms.

Using the above-mentioned features for MoSS it takes about 1 millisecond to compute all maximal common connected substructures for a pair of typical molecules. Of course in some cases it may take much longer, e.g. if the molecules are larger, contain many side-chains or consist of carbon-atoms only. We did not compare MoSS to other MCSS algorithms for MCCSS, because for the typical use cases, there is currently no need for faster algorithms. Computing all pairwise MCSS for the 1,376 of the CDK2 dataset (which is used in the experiments later on) takes about 23 minutes on a dual core 2 GHz computer.

2.3 Estimation of score values

The name maximum-score diversity selection already suggests that besides a significant distance measure (for determining the diversity of the selected subset) the molecules also need a score. Since the goal of most virtual screening approaches is to find potentially active molecules, the score values should correlate with the molecules' real activity. Activities are most often measured by the so-called IC_{50} value, which is the concentration of the compound undergoing tests, at which the activity of a protein in inhibited by 50%. The lower the concentration needed the more active the molecule. Since IC_{50} values are measured in μMol and the concentrations involved can vary over several orders of magnitude, pIC_{50} values are usually used, which are defined as $9-\log_{10}(IC_{50})$. These values are usually between 0 (inactive) and 10 (highly active).

Later on in the experiments either artificial score values will have been created or real, measured activity values are used, because the goal is to show how the algorithms behave under (almost) optimal conditions. However, in practice real activity values are not available (or only for a very small number of compounds) thus they have to be estimated in some way. Unfortunately one – if not *the* – problem of chemoinformatics is activity prediction meaning this is still an unsolved issue. This is one reason why we resorted to real activity data for the experiments, however for the sake of completeness, we shall give a short overview on how activity can be estimated in practice.

The success of any activity prediction method is most often measured by the so-called enrichment factor or the area under the ROC curve. For both measures the whole dataset, consisting of all known active and inactive molecules, is scored with the approach under consideration and the molecules are sorted based on the score. The enrichment factor is then simply the percentage of all active molecules among the first k molecules, the higher the better. There are also more sophisticated measures such as the "BEDROC" score [66], which adds a weighting for the front part of the sorted list.

Current state-of-the-art approaches can be grouped into two-classes: docking and similarity-based. Docking is regarded as the supreme discipline, since it mimics the biochemical processes that happen inside the human body. Most drugs work by inhibiting (or activating) certain proteins. Each protein usually has a distinguished spot – called the *binding pocket* – where small molecules can attach to and trigger a reaction of the protein. The goal of drugs is to either block this pocket so that the original substance cannot attach to the protein any more, preventing any further reactions happening, or the drug is a replacement for the original substance and should stimulate the reaction. This combination of protein binding pocket and molecule is called the *key-keyhole principle*. Docking tries to arrange a molecule inside the binding pocket and then calculates the interactions between the molecule and the protein. The more interactions that are possible, the better the molecule fits and the more efficient it is. Figure 2.6 shows the surface of a protein. The colored molecule is inside the protein's binding pocket. The still unsolved issue with all docking approaches is the "scoring" of the

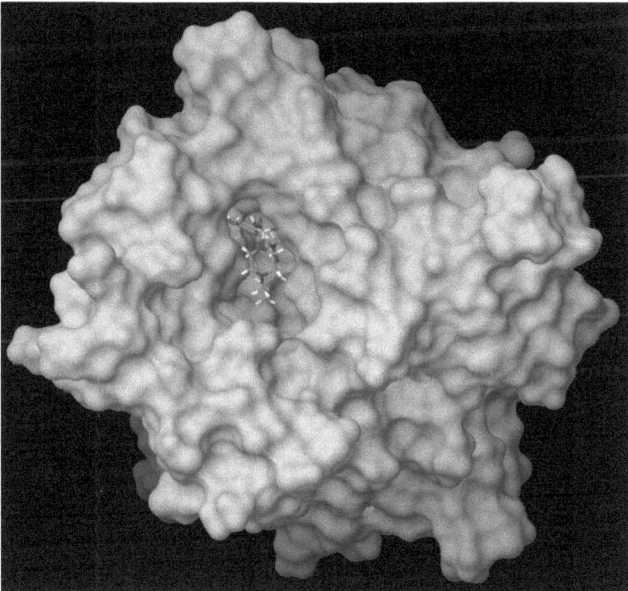

Figure 2.6: A protein with a bound molecule in the binding pocket.

molecule conformations inside the binding pocket, i.e. calculating all relevant interactions of different poses of the same molecule. Moreover, the protein slightly changes its conformation when interactions with molecules occur, which, in turn, affects other interactions. Accurate computations can take several minutes per molecule and even then the correct complex of protein and molecule, which will occur in reality, may not be found. For vHTS usually faster, but less accurate, docking procedures are used, which in many cases are sufficient in order to get an acceptable enrichment. Well-known docking programs are Glide, Gold, Autodock, or FlexX.

The second group does not require a protein, whose structure may not be available in many cases, but works solely on known active molecules. Similar to computing the distances used by MSDS for the diversity objective, similarities to known active molecules are computed. The greater the similarity of an unknown molecule to a known inhibitor, the more likely it is to be active. The algorithms already mentioned in Section 2.1 are used to compute the similarities. In addition to these descriptor- or structure-based approaches there are also so-called *pharmacophore* models. Pharmacophores are three-dimensional abstractions of concrete molecules, where, for example, regions with negative or positive charges, volume constraints, or hydrogen donor or acceptor constraints are substituted for the molecules' atoms and bonds. Figure 2.7 shows a molecule together with several relevant features. The green spheres denote hydrophobic

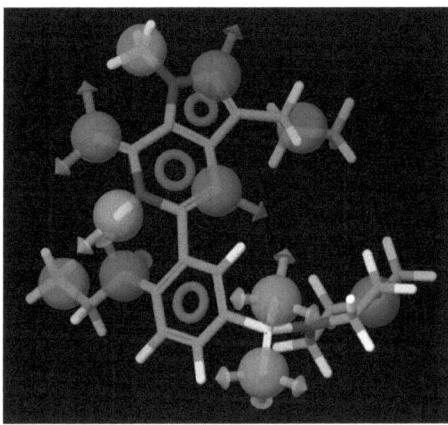

Figure 2.7: The Figure shows a molecule together with the pharmacophore model – indicated by the colored spheres and rings – derived from it.

regions, the red spheres indicate hydrogen acceptors (together with possible directions for the hydrogen bonds), the light blue sphere (left) is a hydrogen donor, the dark blue sphere (right) a positively charged region, and the three aromatic rings systems are symbolized by brown rings.

This three dimensional model (without the molecule) is used to check if unclassified molecules fit spatially. Due to the three-dimensional nature of pharmacophore models, one huge drawback is that a large number of possible conformations of the molecules need to be generated beforehand, because it is very unlikely that the initial conformation (which is more or less arbitrary or a low-energy conformation) has the right orientation and arrangement.

When using such similarity-based approaches for predicting molecules' activities, care must be taken that no measure is chosen that will be used later on to determine the distances for MSDS! It does not make sense to use the same distance measure as a basis for the activity objective, as the distance is subsequently minimized, and when applied to the diversity objective the distance is maximized.

Even though this chapter relates specifically to molecules, we want to stress the fact that MSDS can be applied in any context in which a score and a diversity function is available. Therefore the following chapters discuss MSDS in the more general setting of selecting objects (although some examples still refer to molecules) and the score and distance functions are assumed to be given and appropriately defined.

Chapter 3

Formalization of Maximum-Score Diversity Selection

The concept of MSDS has been explained informally in the introduction, however for further discussion a sound formalization is essential. What has not yet become apparent is the fact that MSDS is a graph-theoretic problem or can at least be modeled as such. Using this kind of representation allows several graph-based concepts and algorithms to be used and avoids developing the theory behind MSDS from scratch. The transformation of the two objectives presented in the introduction into a graph is straightforward: the objects, which should be selected, form the graph's nodes, while their labels are the scores. The distances between all pairs of objects are the labels on the corresponding edges. This results in a complete, undirected and node and edge labeled graph. Figure 3.1 shows a small example of this transformation with four molecules. Subsequently the goal of diversity selection is to choose a fixed-sized clique of nodes that optimizes both objective functions: the score objective on the clique's node labels and the diversity objective on its edge labels.

As was already mentioned, the score objective is easy to define and compute, but it is still unclear how the diversity of the selected subset should be measured. Therefore in the next section several possibilities of defining diversity are discussed. Unfortunately, most sensible definitions lead to $\mathcal{NP}$-hard optimization problems, which is highlighted in Section 3.2.

3.1 Measures for diversity

Of both the objectives involved, maximization of the subset's diversity is by far the most complicated. Not only is the problem of finding an optimal subset computationally infeasible but a proper definition of diversity is not straight-forward. Although users, especially in chemoinformatics, tend to have quite a good idea of what a diverse and active subset should look like, this is of course not suitable for implementation in a computer program.

In most cases diversity is defined based on the distances $d(u, v)$ between the objects under consideration. The further two points are apart, the more dissimilar they are. The challenge is

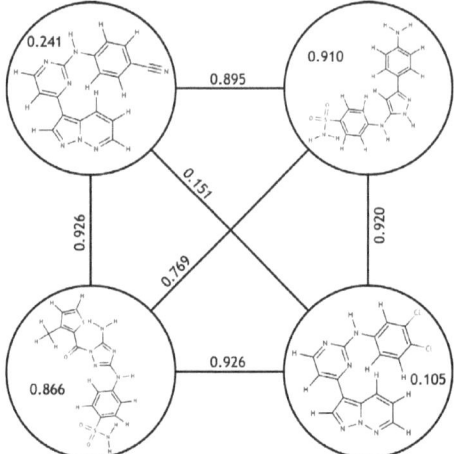

Figure 3.1: Four molecules, which are represented as nodes in a graph. The edges are labeled with the molecules' pairwise distances based on their maximum common substructure. The node labels are the scores.

to employ the pairwise distance relation between two objects for a whole set of objects.

There are (at least) two possible cases when one speaks about diversity of a set. The first is to disperse the selected points "uniformly" over the whole space, regardless of the distribution of all points. This ensures that the available space is covered as evenly as possible. However, this requires a vector space that can somehow be partitioned into equal parts. If only distances between pairs of objects are available and the objects cannot be arranged in a low-dimensional vector space, whereby the distances are obeyed, then this type of diversity cannot be applied.[1] An example of a space covering measure is given in the first definition below.

The second possibility is to select points that resemble the original distribution, i.e. the selected subset approximates the complete set of points. This type of definition does not necessarily require a vector space because the distribution can also be approximated based on the density of points. Density in this context can be defined based on the number of objects in close distance to another object, which only requires distances (see e.g. the DBSCAN clustering algorithm [25]). Depending on which function is used to approximate the original distribution this can lead to cases in which sparsely populated regions are not covered by any point (if applied to a vector space). Examples of such functions are presented below.

Selection of a preferred scenario depends considerably on the application. Completely covering the space will, for example, mean that many points in sparse regions are selected, some of which could be outliers and should therefore not be selected. On the other hand, this kind of point can also be of great interest. Figure 3.2 shows an artificial dataset with a non-uniform distribution of points. In the left part the selected subset tries to cover the whole space, no

---

[1] In principle it is possible to use a very high-dimensional space in which the objects can be arranged properly. However, this space would be useless, since most of the partitions are empty or filled with only one object.

matter how densely populated it is. In the right part the selected points approximate the original distribution to a greater extent.

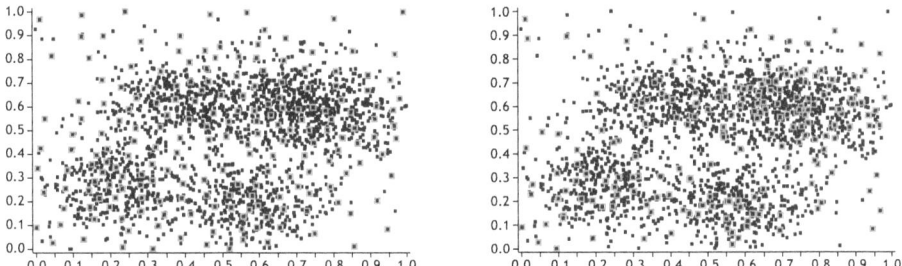

Figure 3.2: Two diverse subsets, covering the whole space in the left diagram, and resembling the original distribution in the right diagram.

In the rest of the thesis we concentrate on diversity in terms of approximating a given distribution, since one assumption of MSDS is that in most cases only pairwise distances are given and that objects cannot be embedded into a low-dimensional vector space. Nevertheless the overview of different diversity functions starts with the hypercube approach that works on vector spaces and tries to cover the complete space.

The hypercube coverage measure

A very intuitive and sensible definition of molecular diversity has been given in [4]. This definition can be translated to any diversity selection problem in which the objects can be described by numeric attributes. Each object from the complete set $I, |I| = n$ is described by a numeric vector of length d that contains several attributes (e.g. molecular weight, charge, volume, etc. for molecules) All these vectors span a d-dimensional hypervolume and each object corresponds to one point in this space. A diverse subset should then cover the space optimally. For this purpose, the hypervolume is partitioned into a set H of k hypercubes $h \in H$ of equal size:

$$h := \{\boldsymbol{x} \in \mathbb{R}^d | \forall i = 0, ..., d-1 : |x_i - z_i| \leq \frac{1}{2}r\} \tag{3.1}$$

$\boldsymbol{z}$ is the center of each hypercube and r the length of the hypercube's edges (which is assumed to be the same in all dimensions). A subset's $S \subseteq I$ diversity is then defined as the fraction of hypercubes that contain at least one object from S.

Definition 9. *The hypercube coverage measure δ_{hc} is defined as*

$$\delta_{hc}(S) = \frac{|\{h \in H : S \cap h \neq \emptyset\}|}{k} \tag{3.2}$$

Intuitively this makes sense: The more hypercubes are covered by the same amount of objects, the better they are distributed over the whole space and therefore form a diverse subset. Figure 3.3 shows two numerical attributes for a set of objects. In terms of the above definition the selected objects in the right 2D plot constitute a more diverse subset than those in the left plot. This hypercube-based definition of diversity also allows for a very easy selection

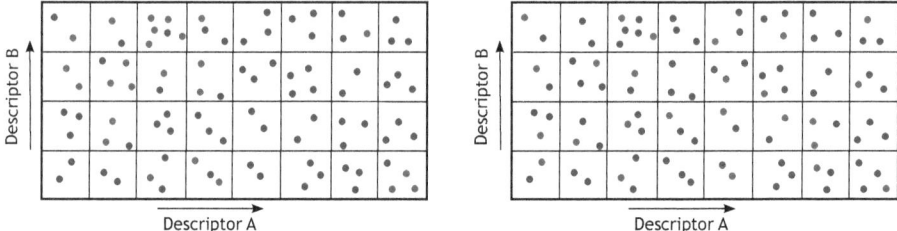

Figure 3.3: Both plots show the same set of objects, characterized by two numerical attributes. The selected subset in the left plot is clearly less diverse than the one in the right plot because its selected points cover substantially less space.

of a diverse subset (compared to the other definitions below). As δ_{hc} is directly influenced by the numbers of occupied hypercubes a simple approach to find an optimal subset is to select an object from each hypercube, preferably objects near their centers, and repeat this process (if necessary) until p objects have been selected.

However, one drawback of this definition is that it only works in vector spaces where the molecules can be arranged in such a way that their positions are in accordance with their original distances. Unfortunately, there are various distance definitions that do not have this property, especially with regard to molecules. One example is the MCSS-based distance presented in Section 2.1. Since only the distances between two structures are known, there is usually no simple way to arrange them in a (low-dimensional) vector space so that the distances inside this space are the same as (or close to) the original substructure-based distances. That this is in fact a problem can be verified by looking at the so-called *agreement measure* [46]. It is defined based on the eigenvalues of the double-centered distance matrix.[2]

Definition 10. *The row mean rm_i is the mean of all values in row i of the $n \times n$ distance matrix $A = (a_{ij})$: $rm_i = \frac{1}{n}\sum_{j=1}^{n} a_{ij}$. The column mean cm_i is defined analogously as $cm_i = \frac{1}{n}\sum_{j=1}^{n} a_{ji}$. The mean m of a matrix A is defined as $m = \frac{1}{n^2}\sum_{i=1}^{n}\sum_{j=1}^{n} a_{ij}$. The double-centered matrix $D = (d_{ij})$ of a matrix A is then defined as $d_{ij} = -0.5(a_{ij} - rm_i - cm_j + m)$.*

Definition 11. *Let λ_i be the n eigenvalues of the double-centered distance matrix D and k be the number of dimensions of the space into which the objects should be embedded. Then the agreement measure α_k is defined as $\alpha_k = \frac{\sum_{i=1}^{k}\lambda_i}{\sum_{i=1}^{n}\lambda_i}$ (since the distances are metric all eigenvalues are non-negative).*

α_k is a value between 0 and 1 indicating the agreement between the original distances and the distances in a k-dimensional Euclidean space. The bigger α_k the better is the agreement.

---

[2]The agreement measure was proposed in the context of multi-dimensional scaling (MDS). MDS is a family of methods for embedding objects into a k-dimensional space such that the original distances are maintained as good as possible. We won't go into detail in this thesis since it is not necessary for further understanding.

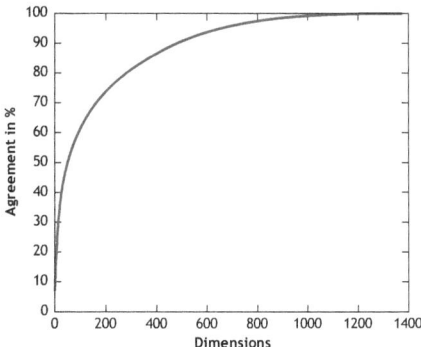

Figure 3.4: The figure shows the agreement measure on the distance matrix of the CDK2 dataset with increasing number of dimensions.

Figure 3.4 shows the agreement measures for the MCSS-based distance matrix computed on CDK2 dataset, which is used in the experiments in Chapter 8. The dataset consists of 1,376 molecules, i.e. the maximum sensible number of dimension is 1,376.

In order to achieve an agreement of e.g. 90% at least 480 dimensions are necessary. This is far too many for the hypercube approach to produce usable results because the number of hypercubes grows exponentially with the number of dimensions. If each dimension in the above example were divided into two parts, this would result in 2^{480} different hypercubes! The possibility of there being more than one object in a hypercube would be extremely low. Therefore selecting any subset of objects would result in a very high diversity. Consequently, for the general case of diversity selection, a definition is required that does not need a vector space, but works solely with the pairwise distances between objects. In the following we assume that all distances are normalized between 0 and 1.

The p-dispersion measure

A more general diversity definition is motivated by the *p-dispersion* or *maxi-min problem* [52, 24, 22]. The goal is to disperse a set of facilities so that the minimum distance between a pair of facilities is maximized.

Definition 12. *The p-dispersion measure δ_d is defined as*

$$\delta_d(S) = \min_{1 \leq i < j \leq p} \{d(u_i, u_j) : u_i, u_j \in S\} \quad (3.3)$$

It is easy to see that only the distances between all pairs of objects are required, regardless of whether they form a vector space or not. Figure 3.5 shows 2,000 randomly distributed points in a 2D space, where the points' distance is their Euclidean distance. The marked points form a subset of 200 objects, which represents a near optimal solution for Equation 3.3. This is not necessarily *the* optimal solution since this cannot be computed efficiently – as we will show in

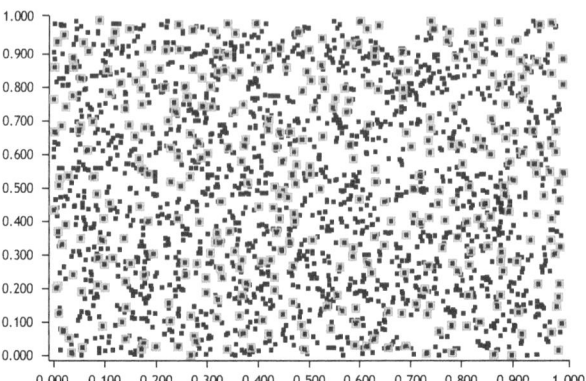

Figure 3.5: A subset of 200 points taken from a set of 2,000 randomly distributed points, which represent a near-optimal solution for the p-dispersion problem.

Section 3.2 – but one that is presumably near the optimum.

Whereas this definition may be perfect for application scenarios where a large minimum distance is crucial, for our case of MSDS in molecules a single pair of (highly active) molecules that are very close to each other will result in a very low diversity even if the remaining molecules cover the molecule space quite evenly. We shall come back to this potential problem in Chapter 7.

The p-dispersion-sum measure

A similar definition, which is used even more often, is the *p-dispersion-sum* or *maximum edge weight clique problem* [59, 57, 52, 6]. Instead of the minimum distance, the sum of all pairwise distances is maximized (which is equivalent to maximizing the average distance).

Definition 13. *The p-dispersion-sum measure is defined as*

$$\delta_{ds}(S) = \sum_{i=1}^{p}\sum_{j=1}^{i-1} d(u_i, u_j) \quad, u_i, u_j \in S \tag{3.4}$$

Intuitively, when optimizing this objective, the selected points are forced away from each other. If a pair of selected objects happens to be quite close, this only slightly affects overall diversity, in contrast to the maxi-min case. However, it seems that in many cases this definition leads to undesirable distributions of points in the space. Figure 3.6 shows the same 2,000 points as above, but now 200 points are selected to optimize Equation 3.4. It is obvious that the selected points are concentrated on the corners of the space and the interior is almost void of any selected point. This is obviously not a diverse distribution. Although the average distance is quite large (about 0.693 in the example), variance is also quite high: inside the corners the distances are very small whereas the inter-corner distances are very large. Even though this is an example in 2D space, which may not be directly transferable into molecule space, it is

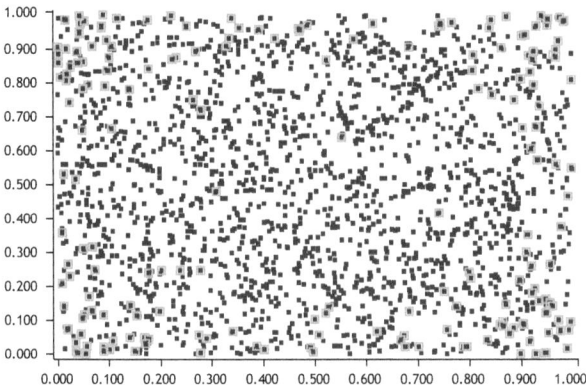

Figure 3.6: A subset of 200 points taken from a set of 2,000 randomly distributed points, representing a near-optimal solution for the p-dispersion-sum problem.

not so unreasonable for molecules close to the borders of the space (supposedly outliers) to be selected. Therefore, this p-dispersion-sum measure may not be very suitable either.

The p-center measure

A different diversity measure can be derived from a problem, known as the *p-center problem* [31, 61]. The function to optimize is the following:

Definition 14. *The p-center measure is defined as*

$$\delta_c(S) = 1 - \max_{1 \leq i \leq n} \min_{1 \leq j \leq p, i \neq j} d(u_i, u_j) \quad , u_i \in I, u_j \in S \tag{3.5}$$

In contrast to the other definitions so far, the p-center function cannot be solely computed with the selected points, rather the whole set of points I needs to be available (for reasons of consistency we do not treat I as second parameter to δ_c but merely rely on the fact that it is given – it remains constant anyway). First, all available points are divided into two sets of selected and unselected points. Next, the minimum distance from each point (selected or not) to any selected point is computed. Since the goal of the p-center problem is to minimize the biggest of these minimal distances, we define the diversity as 1 minus the maximum. Optimizing the p-center problem means choosing the selected points in such a way that each point (from the set of all points!) is as close as possible to at least one selected point. Using the 2D example from above this leads to a very even distribution of selected points over the whole space, see Figure 3.7. One important difference to the other general diversity measures is the complexity of computing the diversity. Whereas the former require $O(p^2)$ computation (since they are a function of the selected objects only), p-center requires $O(p*n)$ computations, which becomes significantly larger, if $p \ll n$ (the standard case in at least the application in vHTS).

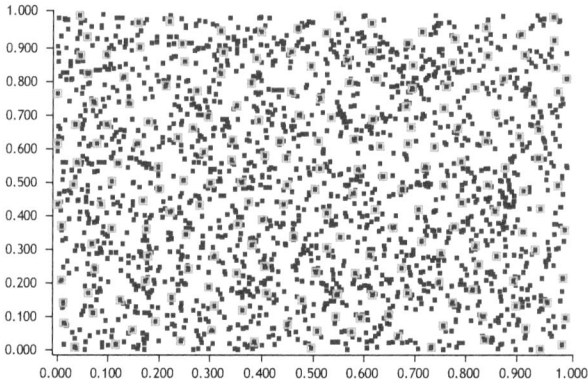

Figure 3.7: A subset of 200 points taken from a set of 2,000 randomly distributed points, representing a near-optimal solution for the p-center problem.

The p-dispersion-min-sum measure

A number of problems can be encountered when applying p-dispersion: a single small distance can ruin diversity; in the p-dispersion-sum measure, many small distances can occur, and the p-center measure is more expensive to compute. However, there is a fourth definition, which involves maximizing the sum of minimal distances to circumvent the above-mentioned deficiencies.

Definition 15. *The p-dispersion-min-sum measure is defined as*

$$\delta_{dms}(S) = \sum_{i=1}^{p} \min_{1 \leq j \leq p, i \neq j} d(u_i, u_j) \quad , u_i, u_j \in S \qquad (3.6)$$

This means that the distances from each point to its nearest neighbor are summed up. Therefore we term it the *p-dispersion-min-sum* problem.

Not only is the influence of few small distances reduced, but also many small distances will heavily influence diversity, as in the corners of Figure 3.6. And indeed, optimizing the same distribution as before but for Equation 3.6 results in a much better coverage of the space (see Figure 3.8). Surprisingly, this definition of diversity, which in many cases appears to work better than the other two, has not found large interest in the research community. Only in the already mentioned article about the hypercube approach [4] is it briefly mentioned as a replacement for non-vector spaces.

To conclude the discussion about diversity we would like to refer briefly to an article from Weitzman [68], in which he proposes another diversity measure:

$$\delta_w(S) = \max_{1 \leq i \leq p}(\delta_w(S - \{u_i\}) + d(u_i, S - \{u_i\})) \qquad (3.7)$$
$$\text{with} \quad d(u_i, Q) = \min_{v \in Q} d(u_i, v)$$

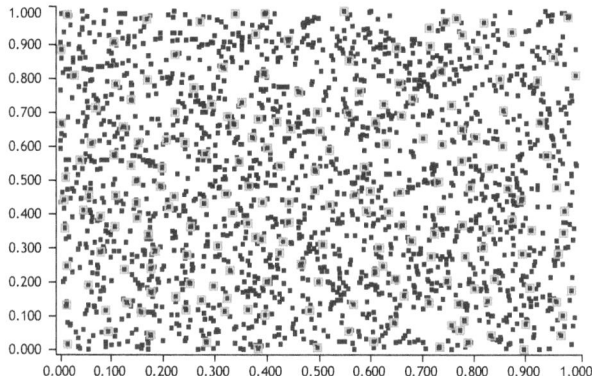

Figure 3.8: A subset of 200 points taken from a set of 2,000 randomly distributed points, which represent a near-optimal solution for the p-dispersion-min-sum problem.

The author argues that this measure is superior over many alternative diversity measures because there are lots of examples where the other measures "fail". The drawback, however, is that this recursively defined measure is unlikely to be efficiently computable. The above definition requires that all possible subsets have to be examined, which is an exponentially large number. Also further publications such as [26] suggest that there is no more efficient way of computing the measure. In this publication the authors describe an application of Weitzman's diversity function: computing merely the diversity for 33 objects (and not even optimizing it) took approximately 11 hours on a relatively modern computer (2005).

Table 3.1 summarizes all the presented diversity measures.

Table 3.1: Summary of all presented diversity measures.

Formula	Complexity	Remarks
Hypercube coverage		
$\delta_{hc}(S) = \frac{|\{h \in H : S \cap h \neq \emptyset\}|}{k}$	$O(n)$	Only for metric spaces
p-dispersion		
$\delta(S) = \min_{1 \leq i < j \leq p} \{d(u_i, u_j)\}$	$O(p^2)$	Also known as *maxi-min* problem
p-dispersion-sum		
$\delta(S) = \sum_{i=1}^{p} \sum_{j=1}^{i-1} d(u_i, u_j)$	$O(p^2)$	Also known as *maximum edge weight clique problem*
p-dispersion-min-sum		
$\delta(S) = \sum_{i=1}^{p} \min_{1 \leq j \leq p, i \neq j} d(u_i, u_j)$	$O(p^2)$	
p-center		
$\delta(S) = 1 - \max_{1 \leq i \leq n} \min_{1 \leq j \leq p, i \neq j} d(u_i, u_j)$	$O(p * n)$	
Weitzman		
$\delta(S) = \max_{1 \leq i \leq p} (\delta(S - \{u_i\}) + d(u_i, S - \{u_i\}))$	$O(2^n)$	Supposedly not efficiently computable

There may be well be other possibilities of defining diversity measures (e.g. the size of the minimum spanning tree for the selected nodes). However, in this thesis only the presented p-dispersion measures are further evaluated. p-dispersion and p-dispersion-sum are commonly used measures (at least in literature) as is p-center. However, as was pointed out before, p-dispersion-min-sum may have several advantages over the former measures. All four measures are therefore compared in the experiments in Chapter 7. Weitzman's diversity measure is not discussed any further for obvious reasons.

3.2 Maximum-score diversity selection is $\mathcal{NP}$-hard

Even if the above definitions of diversity lead to different solutions (in the 2D case) they all have one thing in common: finding a subset that maximizes the diversity function is an $\mathcal{NP}$-hard problem. This means that it is (presumably) computationally infeasible to find a guaranteed optimal solution for all but very small problem instances. State-of-the-art exact algorithms for the p-dispersion-sum problem currently find solutions for only less than 100 objects (see e.g. [64]). However, in real world scenarios such as chemoinformatics, selecting 1,000 out of 10,000 molecules is a fairly common problem size. Therefore only heuristic approaches can be used to find near-optimal subsets of objects. In the remainder of this chapter we sketch the $\mathcal{NP}$-completeness proofs for the various diversity definitions introduced in the previous section.[3] The first part is a repetition of existing proofs for the pure diversity selection problem (without scores/node labels) and in the second part we present the proof for MSDS.

$\mathcal{NP}$-completeness proofs involve finding a suitable transformation of a known $\mathcal{NP}$-complete problem to the problem under consideration. Fortunately there is a huge collection of problems to choose from when searching for a suitable reduction, which have been proven to be $\mathcal{NP}$-complete. ([27] is an excellent source). Since diversity selection is usually modeled as a graph problem, it makes sense to use other graph problems for the reduction.

Let's start with the p-dispersion problem.

Theorem 2. *The p-dispersion problem, i.e. deciding if the complete graph G contains a subset $S \subseteq V$ with exactly p nodes such that the clique defined by S satisfies $\delta_d(S) = d$ for any value d, is $\mathcal{NP}$-complete.*

Proof. Erkut [24] used *CLIQUE* as a starting point for reduction. Recall that the clique problem determines whether a graph G has a clique of size p or greater, i.e. a subgraph G_1 with p or more nodes all of which are connected with each other. The transformation from CLIQUE to p-dispersion is fairly straightforward: G is extended into a complete graph G' by adding the missing edges where all edges also occurring in G are given an edge label of 1, all other edges not in G are given a label of 0, see Figure 3.9. It is clear that the transformation can be performed in polynomial time in the number of nodes. The resulting graph G' is a restricted

---
[3]Readers not familiar with the theory around $\mathcal{NP}$-completeness may find the short summary in appendix A useful.

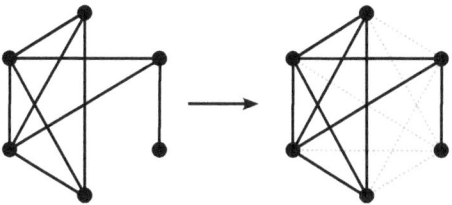

Figure 3.9: Transformation from an arbitrary graph to a complete graph. The edges of the original graph are in black and all have a label of 1.

instance of the general p-dispersion problem in that there are only two different edge labels, 0 and 1. Now, G contains a clique of size p if and only if G' contains a subset S of p nodes with $\delta_d(S) = 1$ (i.e. only edges from the original graph G are used, otherwise δ_d would be 0), see Figure 3.10a. Therefore if a polynomial-time algorithm existed for finding such a subset then the $\mathcal{NP}$-complete CLIQUE problem could also be solved in polynomial time, which is a contradiction. Consequently, the p-dispersion problem must be $\mathcal{NP}$-complete, too. □

The same proof can also be applied to the p-dispersion-sum or maximum edge weight clique problem.

Theorem 3. *The p-dispersion-sum problem, i.e. deciding if the complete graph G contains a subset $S \subseteq V$ with exactly p nodes such that the clique defined by S satisfies $\delta_{ds}(S) = d$ for any value d, is $\mathcal{NP}$-complete.*

Proof. The second name already indicates its relation to the clique problem: In addition to finding a clique of size k the clique must also be one with maximal edge weight sum. Using the same transformation as above (setting the labels of all edges in G' that also occur in G to 1 and all others to 0) the question is now, if G' contains a subset of p nodes with $\delta_{ds}(S) = \frac{p*(p-1)}{2}$. If such a subset existed, it would form a clique of size p in the original graph G, see Figure 3.10b. Again, this shows that no polynomial time algorithm for p-dispersion-sum can exist, either. □

Finally, also the proof for the novel p-dispersion-min-sum measure is similar.

Theorem 4. *The p-dispersion-min-sum problem, i.e. deciding if the complete graph G contains a subset $S \subseteq V$ with exactly p nodes such that the clique defined by S satisfies $\delta_{dms}(S) = d$ for any value d, is $\mathcal{NP}$-complete.*

Proof. Once again, all edges in G' that are also present in G are assigned a label of 1 and all other edges are labeled with 0. A p-subset of nodes from G' with $\delta_{dms} = p$ corresponds to a clique of size p in the original graph G, see Figure 3.10c. Therefore p-dispersion-min-sum is also $\mathcal{NP}$-complete. □

Note that the marked edges in Figures 3.10a and 3.10c are not the only solutions. For p-dispersion any bold edge can be selected, for p-dispersion-min-sum only two edges can be counted in δ_{dms} (but multiple times) if a pair of nodes are their mutual nearest neighbors.

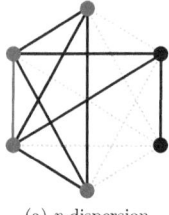 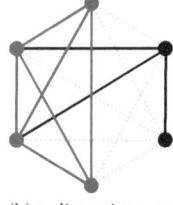 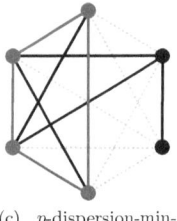

(a) *p*-dispersion (b) *p*-dispersion-sum (c) *p*-dispersion-min-sum

Figure 3.10: The red nodes are solutions to the various *p*-dispersion problems and the red edges are the ones that contribute to the corresponding diversity functions.

The *p*-center problem differs slightly from the *p*-dispersion problems because it is defined on both sets of nodes, the selected *and* the unselected ones. Therefore, the $\mathcal{NP}$-completeness proof (taken from [36]) is based on the dominating set problem [27], which also involves two sets of nodes. The dominating set problem asks whether a graph $G = (V, E)$ contains a subset $S \subseteq V$ of size *p* so that for all nodes $x \in V - S$ there exists a node $y \in S$ and an edge $\{x, y\} \in E$. This means that the graph's nodes are divided into selected and unselected nodes and each unselected node has at least one selected neighbor. Figure 3.11 shows a graph with two different dominating sets of size three (the minimum size for this graph).

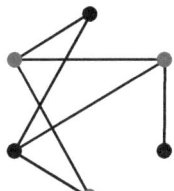 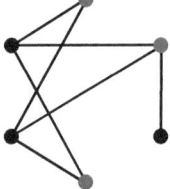

Figure 3.11: Two different dominating sets of size three.

Theorem 5. *The p-center problem, i.e. deciding if the complete graph G contains a subset $S \subseteq V$ with exactly p nodes such that the clique defined by S satisfies $\delta_c(S) = d$ for any value d, is $\mathcal{NP}$-complete.*

Proof. The reduction of the dominating set problem to the *p*-center problem is similar to the transformations for *p*-dispersion. The original graph G is extended into a complete graph $G' = (V, E')$ where each edge in E' that also exists in E is assigned a label of one, and each additional edge not in E is assigned a label of two. Supposing that we are able to find a subset S of size *p* in G' with $\delta_c(S) = 1$ – thus only the original edges from G are used – then this subset would also be a dominating set in G. On the other hand, if $\delta_c(S) = 2$, i.e. at least one of the additional edges is used, then G does not contain a dominating set of size *p*. This is demonstrated in Figure 3.12. The left graph contains a 3-center with $\delta_c(S) = 1$, whereas the right graph contains a 2-center but has to use some additional edges with length two and therefore has $\delta_c(S) = 2$. Hence, the algorithm for p-center can also solve the dominating

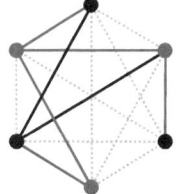 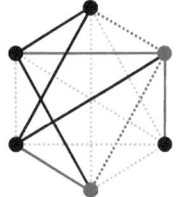

Figure 3.12: The left graph shows a 3-center using only edges of length one whereas the right graph shows a 2-center that must also use edges of length two.

set problem and if this algorithm ran in polynomial time, then the dominating set problem would also be solvable in polynomial time, which is a contradiction. Consequently, the p-center problem also has to be $\mathcal{NP}$-complete. □

The figure also shows the difference between the dominating set problem and the similar maximum independent set problem, which increases in significance when we discuss an algorithm for optimizing the p-center measure in Section 6.2: the former allows a selected node to also have selected neighbors (such as in the left graph of the figure) whereas for the latter this is forbidden (such as in the right graph). A subset $V_I \subseteq V$ is called an *independent set* if $\forall x, y \in V_I, x \neq y : \{x, y\} \notin E$, i.e. there is no edge between any pair of nodes in V_I. A maximum independent set is an independent set V_I such that no larger independent set exists. This is equivalent to a clique in the inverse graph (a graph in which edges and non-edges are exchanged) and vice versa. Therefore the independent set problem is $\mathcal{NP}$-complete, too.

The theorems above only considered the decision variants of the diversity problems, i.e. deciding if a subset of nodes with a certain diversity value exists. However, in MSDS we want to find the optimum subset, i.e. the one that maximizes any of the diversity functions. Since the decision problems are already $\mathcal{NP}$-complete the corresponding optimization problems are at least as complicated to solve and are therefore $\mathcal{NP}$-hard.

So far the results mentioned above only hold for the task of pure diversity selection, i.e do not take the activity objective into account. However, reducing any of the pure problems to the multi-objective MSDS is not a complex procedure.

Theorem 6. *MSDS with any of the four presented diversity measures is an $\mathcal{NP}$-hard optimization problem.*

Proof. For example, the $\mathcal{NP}$-hard p-dispersion-sum optimization problem can be transformed to MSDS in linear time. This can be accomplished by setting all node labels to the same constant value c. This ensures that only the edge labels have an influence on the function to be optimized, and a solution to this (special) MSDS is a solution to the corresponding p-dispersion/p-center problem. □

The same construction is applicable to all other p-dispersion and p-center measures. Note, that this does *not* imply that *all* instances of MSDS are hard to solve. For example, instances where node labels are much larger than edge labels, such that the optimized function is completely dominated by the node labels, are easy to solve. However, MSDS in general, without any further restrictions on the node and edge labels, is $\mathcal{NP}$-hard.

In this chapter we have discussed several measures for diversity and shown that pure diversity selection and its extension to MSDS are both $\mathcal{NP}$-hard optimization problems, which makes it impossible to find guaranteed optimal subsets for more than about a hundred objects. Nevertheless we are interested in good solutions, even if they may not be optimal. Therefore the next chapter discusses various types of optimization problems and general approaches to finding near-optimal solutions.

Chapter 4

Multi-objective Optimization

As we have already explained in the introduction, maximum-score diversity selection belongs to the class of multi-objective optimization problems. Since multi-objective optimization is a special case of general optimization, a short introduction to the subject is given in Section 4.1. Optimization can be grouped into several classes, the most important for this thesis being linear optimization (Section 4.2), combinatorial optimization (Section 4.3), and multi-objective optimization (Section 4.4). The latter two classes play particularly important roles in MSDS.

4.1 General optimization

Optimization is the process of finding the maximum or minimum value of a mathematical function f

$$f : X \to \mathbb{R} \qquad (4.1)$$

where X can be almost any set of objects. Examples are $\mathbb{R}^k$ if the variables take on real values or sets with only a very restricted number of values, e.g. $\{0,1\}^k$ in the case of binary optimization problems. The function f is often also referred to as *objective function*. The minimum and maximum $\boldsymbol{x}_{min}/\boldsymbol{x}_{max}$ are defined as

$$f(\boldsymbol{x}_{min}) \leq f(\boldsymbol{x}) \quad \forall \boldsymbol{x} \in X \qquad (4.2)$$

and

$$f(\boldsymbol{x}_{max}) \geq f(\boldsymbol{x}) \quad \forall \boldsymbol{x} \in X \qquad (4.3)$$

respectively. Usually, optimization problems are *constrained*, which means that the values x_i of a solution (optimal or not) may not take arbitrary values from set X. Constraints can be formulated as equalities or inequalities, e.g. that certain x_i must be in a restricted range of X, that the sum of all x_i is smaller or greater than some fixed value, or even more complicated formulas. In principle each $\boldsymbol{x} \in X$ is a solution to the problem, however one is interested in only a small subset of X. Solutions to an optimization problem that do not satisfy all constraints are called *infeasible* and can be discarded. If one of the remaining feasible solutions optimizes

f it is referred to as an *optimal* solution.

Depending on the nature of X, f, and the constraints, optimization problems are grouped into a number of different categories, some of which are:

Nonlinear Programming This is a very general class of optimization problems (the term "programming" has historical reasons and was at first not related to computer programs), where X is usually $\mathbb{R}^k$ and the x_i in f and the constraints can occur in linear and nonlinear combinations. Nonlinear problems are usually hard to solve.

Linear Programming (LP) Probably the most popular type of optimization problems, in which X is a subset of $\mathbb{R}^k$, f consists of a linear combination of the x_i only, and all constraints are also linear.

Quadratic Programming (QP) The objective function contains linear and quadratic terms of x_i, but the constraints are still linear.

Integer Programming (IP) These problems are a restriction of linear optimization problems, where X consists of integer values only: $X = \mathbb{Z}^k$. This restriction makes most problems much harder than linear problems.

Binary Integer Programming (BIP) A further restriction of X to $\{0,1\}^k$.

Combinatorial optimization If all solutions belong to a discrete set, the search for an optimal solution is called combinatorial optimization. In principle the optimum can be found by enumerating all elements of the finite set X, which is not possible for LP or QP problems. BIP can also be seen as a special case of combinatorial optimization.

Multi-objective optimization The optimization problem does not have a single-objective function, it is rather that there are several criteria that need to be optimized at the same time (f is extended to a vector function). Usually the objectives are conflicting and cannot be optimized simultaneously.

There are many more categories into which an optimization problem can fall, but the above are the most commonly used. MSDS is certainly a multi-objective problem and its natural formulation makes it a combinatorial optimization problem, as the selected objects are from a discrete and finite set and so are all possible solutions. However, LP and BIP also play a role in the following discussion. Therefore, in the next sections linear and combinatorial optimization are described first in some detail before introducing multiple objectives.

4.2 Linear optimization

MSDS is clearly not a general linear optimization problem, because an object is either selected or not, i.e. the variables are binary and not real. Therefore, solution techniques for linear programming cannot be applied directly to MSDS. However, it is possible to derive bounds for several combinatorial problems by using a method called *linear programming relaxation*. The integer constraints on the variables are dropped and the linear programming problem is solved. Its solution is usually different from the corresponding integer programming solution. More precisely the LP solutions are equal or better than the corresponding IP solutions. Therefore the former can be used to derive bounds for the latter. This process is described in more detail in the next section. However, in order to apply this method a basic understanding of linear programming is necessary.

As we already described above, a linear optimization problem consists of a function f, which is a linear combination of all variables x_i and several linear equalities or inequalities as constraints. Formally, this is written as

$$\text{Optimize} \quad f = \boldsymbol{c}^T \boldsymbol{x} \tag{4.4}$$
$$\text{Subject to} \quad A\boldsymbol{x} \leq \boldsymbol{b} \tag{4.5}$$

A simple example with two variables (inspired by [48]) is

$$\begin{aligned} \text{Maximize} \quad & x_1 + x_2 \\ \text{Subject to} \quad & x_1 \geq 0 \\ & x_2 \geq 0 \\ & x_2 - x_1 \leq 1 \\ & x_1 + 6x_2 \leq 15 \\ & 4x_1 - x2 \leq 9 \end{aligned}$$

For a better understanding, the above problem can be visualized graphically. The constraints (formulated as inequalities) define a polygon inside which all feasible solutions lie, see Figure 4.1. The optimal solution is subsequently the one that is inside the polygon and maximizes the objective function. The maximum value lies in the direction of the vector $\boldsymbol{c}$ that defines the coefficients for x_i, which is $(1, 1)$ in the example. In cases with two or three variables graphical construction of the optimal solution is a simple procedure. All points on a line that is perpendicular to the coefficient vector $\boldsymbol{c}$ have equal objective function values. The farther away from the origin these lines are, the greater the objective function value becomes. Therefore we are seeking the last intersection of such a line with the polygon of feasible solutions Figure 4.2 show three such lines, the bold one being the one with the optimum value. The optimum solution is the right corner point of the polygon at the coordinates $(2.76, 2.04)$. The objective function value at this point is 4.8.

The example has one single optimal solution. However, linear programming problems may have more than one solution, if one of the edges of the polygon (in the two-dimensional case) is orthogonal to the direction of $\boldsymbol{c}$, or no solution if the feasible area is empty. The objective function may also be unbounded if the polygon is open in the direction of $\boldsymbol{c}$ (e.g. if the last two constraints in the example are dropped).

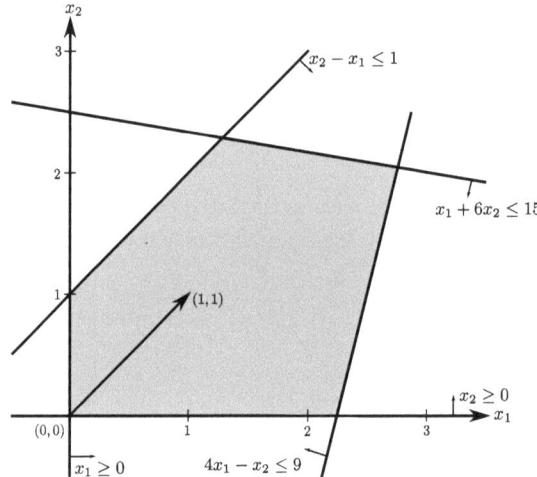

Figure 4.1: Feasible area of the linear programming example that is formed by the constraint inequalities. The optimum point lies in the direction of the coefficient vector $\mathbf{c}$.

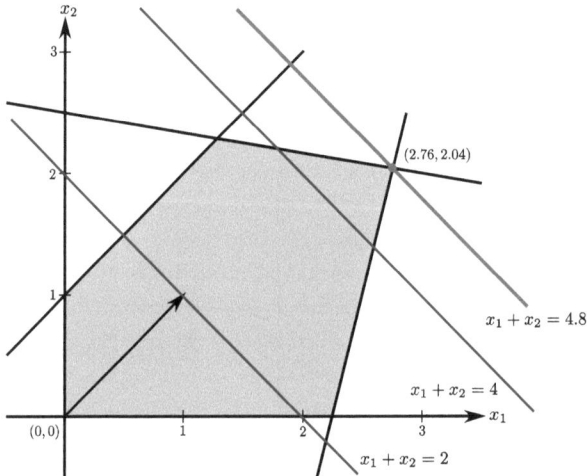

Figure 4.2: The three colored lines indicate values where $x_1 + x_2$ is constant. The intersection with the feasible area and the line farthest away from the origin is the optimal solution.

Even if solving linear programs in two or three dimensions may work in this visual way, it cannot be used if more variables are involved. And almost all linear programming problems consist of many more variables than just two or three. One standard algorithm is the so-called *simplex method*, which was invented by the American mathematician Georg Dantzig in 1947. Today it is presumably still the most popular way of solving linear optimization problems. Although there is no guarantee that it can solve any problem in acceptable time — there are in fact instances that lead to exponential runtimes [37] — it can handle almost all realistic cases with even thousands of variables and constraints efficiently.

4.3 Combinatorial optimization

Still, the question remains, how linear programming is related to maximum-score diversity selection, which is a combinatorial optimization problem. For this, we first have to inspect MSDS more thoroughly. We want to accomplish the following:

1. Maximize the score of the selected objects. Suppose each object u_i has a corresponding indicator value given by $x_i \in \{0,1\}$ with a value of one if u_i is selected and zero if not. Each object has a fixed score $\sigma(u_i)$, therefore we can write this objective function as $\sum_{i=1}^{n} x_i \, \sigma(u_i)$. This is obviously a linear function in the x_i.

2. Maximize the diversity of the subset. Assuming that the diversity function to be optimized is δ_{ds} (p-dispersion-sum, see Equation 3.4) then this objective function can be written as $\sum_{i=1}^{n} \sum_{j=i}^{i-1} x_i \, x_j \, d(u_i, u_j)$.

Unfortunately the second objective function is not linear any more, so we cannot use it in this way. However, since x_i are restricted to either zero or one, the product $x_i * x_j$ is also either zero or one. We can therefore replace the product with an auxiliary variable $x_{ij} \in \{0, 1\}$ and add a constraint $x_{ij} - 0.5(x_i + x_j) = 0$ (this is similar to a set of inequalities used in e.g. [56, 64]). Adding the general constraint that exactly p objects must be selected results in the following system of equations:

$$\text{Maximize} \quad \sum_{i=1}^{n} x_i \, \sigma(u_i) + \sum_{i=1}^{n} \sum_{j=1}^{i-1} x_{ij} \, d(u_i, u_j) \tag{4.6}$$

$$\text{Subject to} \quad x_{ij} - 0.5(x_i + x_j) = 0, \forall i, j \in [1..n] \tag{4.7}$$

$$\sum_{i=1}^{n} x_i = p \tag{4.8}$$

$$x_i \in \{0, 1\} \tag{4.9}$$

$$x_{ij} \in \{0, 1\} \tag{4.10}$$

The restriction to values from $\{0, 1\}$ makes this an integer program, precisely a binary integer program. Coming back to our example from the previous section, the integer version of the linear optimization problem problem can be seen in Figure 4.3. Instead of the complete polygon

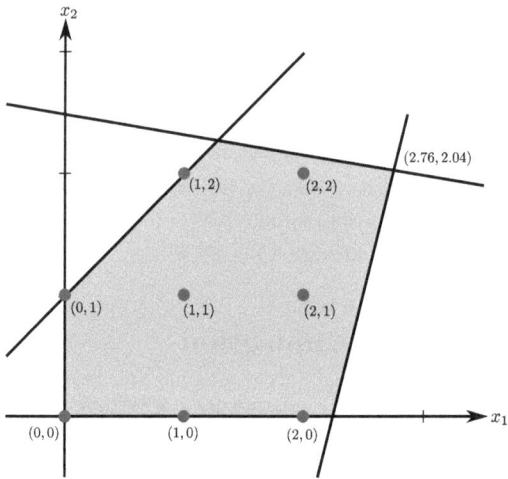

Figure 4.3: Integer version of the linear programming example from the previous section. The feasible solutions are the dots inside the feasible area of the corresponding linear program.

formed by the constraints the feasible solutions are now represented by only a very small subset of points inside the polygon. Obviously, it would be a coincidence, if the solution of the linear program is the same as the solution for the corresponding integer version. Hence the questions arises, how an integer program can be solved. Looking at our small example one is tempted to take the linear solution and round the values to the nearest integers. However, even in the example this does not work as $(3,2)$ is outside the feasible region of even the linear problem. Even if rounding was possible, what value would we choose in our MSDS application if, for example, some x_i are given a value of 0.5? Does this mean that the object is selected (i.e. rounding it to one) or that is not selected (i.e. rounding it to zero)? These and other problems associated with rounding LP solutions can be found in [29]. In short, just rounding the LP solutions does not work and therefore other ways of solving integer programming problems have to be found.

But why does one even try to round the solution of the linear program and not use an algorithm for the integer program? The reason is that unfortunately (binary) integer programs in general are $\mathcal{NP}$-hard [27] and therefore cannot be solved efficiently (in contrast to linear programs), especially with regard to instances with several thousand objects such as in early drug discovery.

However, one thing that we can do — and which is actually quite often done in practice — is not to use the solution components of the LP problem but merely the optimal function value associated with the solution. This process is commonly called the *linear programming relaxation* (LP-relaxation) of the integer programming problem. The reason for applying this process is that the linear programming solution tells us at least one important thing: solutions to the integer problem cannot be better than the linear solution(s). This is quite obvious from our example, since all feasible integer solutions lie inside the polygon and thus are nearer to the origin than the optimal linear solution. Therefore the LP-relaxation gives us an upper bound on the objective function value of the integer problem. And if we have an approximate solution to the problem (computed by some other means) we can compare it to the LP-relaxation's objective function value and get an impression of how good our solution is.

For the LP-relaxation the integer constraints on the variables are dropped. For our example this leads to the following linear program:

$$\text{Maximize} \quad \sum_{i=1}^{n} x_i \, \sigma(u_i) + \sum_{i=1}^{n}\sum_{j=1}^{i-1} x_{ij} \, d_{ij}$$

$$\text{Subject to} \quad x_{ij} - 0.5(x_i + x_j) = 0, \forall i,j \in [1..n]$$

$$\sum_{i=1}^{n} x_i = p$$

$$x_i \in [0,1]$$

$$x_{ij} \in [0,1]$$

However, solving this LP leads to unexpected results. Since the objective function is to be maximized and the number of selected edges, i.e. the x_{ij}, is not constrained directly but only indirectly via the first constraint, the solution will contain many $x_{ij} > 0$ where only one of the adjacent nodes x_i or x_j is selected. This is of course wrong, because an edge may only be counted if both nodes are selected. This problem can (at least partially) be addressed by adding two additional constraints:

$$x_i - x_{ij} \geq 0$$
$$x_i - x_{ji} \geq 0$$

This ensures that an edge is only given a non-zero weight if both adjacent nodes also have non-zero values. Solutions to this extended LP still suffer from fractional values for x_i and x_{ij}, and even worse in most cases all nodes and edges have the same non-zero value. Thus it is totally unclear, which nodes have been selected. There is, however, one result from LP optimization that could in principle be used: the optimal objective function value. Since the integer version of a maximization problem always produces smaller (or at most equal) solutions the LP value is an upper bound to the IP problem. This would allow for an estimation about the quality of IP approximations (that have been found by other methods). If their values are close to the optimal LP value then they are presumably quite near the real optimum. Unfortunately, applying this approach to some of the datasets used in the experiments always resulted in LP function values, which were very close or even equal to 1 (for values normalized between 0 and 1). The results of the heuristic approaches suggest that this upper bound is not concise enough to be used in practice. Therefore we have not performed any more experiments with LP relaxation.

4.4 Multiple objectives

So far we have only dealt with problems that have one single function to be optimized. However, in reality many problems consist of more than one objective:

- Suppose you want to buy a new car. It should be really fast but you want to spend as little money as possible. Clearly, the faster the car should be, the more money you have to spend. So where is the best trade-off between the two objectives? How much money is 10 km/h of top speed worth (to you)?

- In portfolio selection the expected gain should be as high as possible but the risk in losing money should be minimized. Usually, it is not possible to achieve both at the same time. Therefore the question is, what is the best selection of stocks?

- Students need to take several courses in university. Being students, they want to have as little work as possible, still get good grades and also take courses that are interesting and prepare them well for the future. What is the best selection of courses to optimize these three objectives.

These three simple examples show one important (if not the most important) aspect of problems with multiple objectives: typically the objectives involved are conflicting, i.e. optimizing one objective (e.g. speed of the car) leads to a deterioration of the other objective(s) (e.g. money to be spent). Therefore it is not possible to find one optimal solution but only several "suboptimal" solutions each of which involves a certain drawback in one or more of the objectives.

Coming back to the car example, the possible choices of cars can be arranged in a two-dimensional plot where both axes define one objective, see Figure 4.4. Each point in the diagram represents a car with its top speed and its price. The optimal car would cost you no

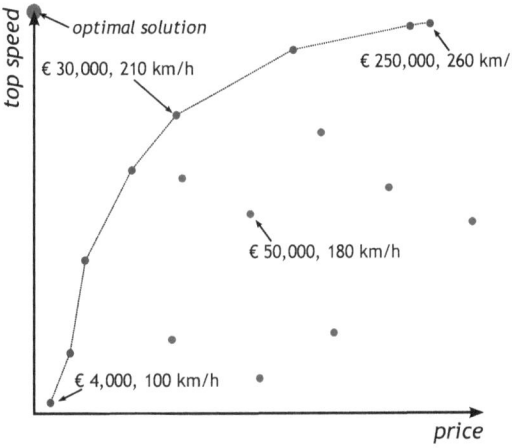

Figure 4.4: Possible solutions for the car example characterized by price and top speed.

money and have the highest top speed. This car would be in the top left point of the diagram, but obviously this kind of car does not exist. Therefore all realistic cars are somewhere below the optimal solution. They can be grouped into two classes, indicated by the red and green points. The marked red point in the center of the diagram corresponds to a car that costs € 50,000 and has a top speed of 180 km/h. However, there is at least one other car that is cheaper *and* drives faster at the same time: the one that costs € 30,000 and has a top speed of 210 km/h. The same is true for all other red cars and in any case there is another car that is better in both objectives. However, for the green cars, no such choices exist. There are cars that are cheaper or faster, but in all cases they are either slower or more expensive, respectively. For these two classes, the terms *dominated* and *non-dominated* have been defined. The green cars dominate the red cars and are themselves non-dominated by any other car. The set of non-dominated solutions is also called the *Pareto front* (named after an Italian economist who first described this concept in the 19th century), since its elements form a kind of wave-front that tries to converge to the (utopian) optimal solution. Intuitively, no one would choose a red car, therefore the non-dominated solutions are the ones that are interesting in multi-objective optimization problems. What is also fairly obvious from the example, is the fact that the last decision, which of the non-dominated solutions is chosen in the end, depends on the individual human (providing no further constraints have been modeled in the problem).

Multi-objective optimization problems are not restricted to two or three objectives as in the examples, but in principle an arbitrary number of objectives can be involved. Therefore a general definition for multi-objective optimization problems and the Pareto-concept is required. A multi-objective optimization problem can be written formally as

$$\text{Maximize } \boldsymbol{f}(\boldsymbol{x}) = (f_1(\boldsymbol{x}), f_2(\boldsymbol{x}), ..., f_k(\boldsymbol{x}))$$
$$\text{Subject to } \boldsymbol{x} \in F$$

where the $f_i : X \to \mathbb{R}$ are the objective functions and $\boldsymbol{x} = (x_1, x_2, ..., x_n)^T$ is an element of $F \subset X$, the set of possible or feasible solutions. Similar to linear programs, the definition only covers maximization problems, but a minimization problem (or any combination thereof) can easily be reformulated as a pure maximization problem by changing the signs of the f_i accordingly.

4.4.1 The dominance relation

Using the objective function values for a pair of solutions, the *dominance relation* can now be defined as follows:

Definition 16. *A solution $\boldsymbol{x} \in F$ dominates a solution $\boldsymbol{y} \in F$, in short $\boldsymbol{x} \succ \boldsymbol{y}$, iff $f_i(\boldsymbol{x}) \geq f_i(\boldsymbol{y})$ for all $i = 1, 2, ..., k$ and $f_j(\boldsymbol{x}) > f_j(\boldsymbol{y})$ for at least one index j.*

This means, $\boldsymbol{x}$ is strictly better than $\boldsymbol{y}$ in at least one of the objectives and has equal values in the remaining objectives. A feasible solution $\boldsymbol{x} \in F$ is called *non-dominated* or *Pareto optimal* if no other $y \in F$ exists for which $y \succ x$. The Pareto front consists of all non-dominated solutions.

Besides this rather intuitive concept of Pareto dominance, there is also the weaker concept of ϵ-dominance [42].

Definition 17. *A solution x ϵ-dominates a solution y, for short $x \succ_\epsilon y$, for some $\epsilon > 0$ if $(1+\epsilon) * f_i(x) \geq f_i(y)$ for all $i = 1, 2, ..., k$.*

The main implications of this definition are twofold. First, the set of ϵ-non-dominated solutions depends on the choice of ϵ and also on the order in which solutions are added to the set (or removed from it)! Since a solution's dominated region is now larger than for pure Pareto dominance, many Pareto optimal solutions are now ϵ-dominated and are not considered for the Pareto front any more. Figure 4.5 shows the Pareto dominated region of a solution on the left and the ϵ-dominated region of the same solution on the right. If solution x were chosen then

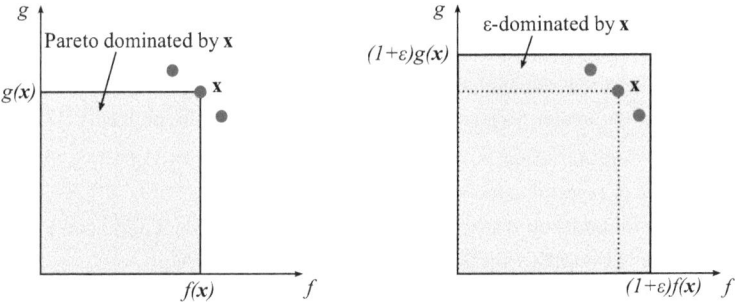

Figure 4.5: The two diagrams show the Pareto dominated region of a solution on the left and the ϵ-dominated region on the right.

the other two solutions would be ϵ-dominated. If any of the other two solutions were chosen first, then x would be ϵ-dominated. Therefore the set of ϵ-dominating solutions depends on the order of selecting solutions. With this definition of dominance solutions can even occur that are not Pareto-optimal, if the dominated region includes Pareto-optimal solutions. Thus, two different kinds of sets can be defined for the ϵ-dominance relation. The ϵ-*approximate* Pareto set contains solutions that are ϵ-dominating but are not necessarily Pareto-optimal, whereas the ϵ-Pareto set contains only Pareto-optimal solutions, i.e. a subset of all non-dominated solutions.

The second implication of ϵ-dominance is of practical interest, since the ϵ-Pareto set is usually much smaller than the Pareto set (depending on the choice of ϵ). This can be of interest if the number of non-dominated solutions is very large. On the one hand, optimization algorithms, especially population based algorithms, which will be covered in Chapter 5, have to be used carefully in order to approximate the whole Pareto front and not only parts of it. Using ϵ-dominance can prevent the algorithm from concentrating too much on densely populated regions of the front [42]. On the other hand, the reduced set of solutions makes it easier for the user to select a solution – if he is presented only a few dozens instead of several hundreds (or even more) solutions.

4.4.2 Ranking Pareto front approximations by indicator functions

The true Pareto front with respect to real world optimization problems is usually not known; the sole task of optimization algorithms is to find a good approximation of the Pareto front. One fundamental problem is the comparison of different approximations. Which set of solutions is the best one? For many cases, such as the left and middle example in Figure 4.6, the answer is easy and can be determined by extending the Pareto dominance relation from pairs of solution to complete sets. Let Ψ denote the set of all Pareto front approximations (containing only pairwise non-dominated solutions). Subsequently a set of solutions $A \in \Psi$ dominates a set $B \in \Psi$ if all solutions from A dominate all solutions from B:

$$A \succ B \Leftrightarrow \forall x \in A, \forall y \in B : x \succ y \tag{4.11}$$

This concept can easily be justified with the left and middle diagrams of Figure 4.6. Clearly in both cases set A is better than the solutions in set B. However, this pure binary indicator

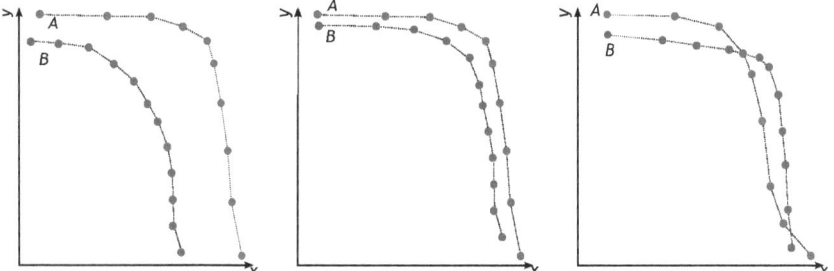

Figure 4.6: Set A is clearly a better approximation of the true Pareto front than B in the left and middle diagram, whereas in the right it is unclear at first sight, which one is better.

cannot distinguish between the left and middle case, where in the latter the set B is only slightly worse, and does not make any statement for the right case in which neither set A completely dominates set B nor the other way round. Therefore more sophisticated measures are needed. Most popular are so-called unary quality indicators that do not compare a pair of sets but instead compute a real number for each set: $I : \Psi \to \mathbb{R}$. Such a unary measure I should satisfy several properties ([71]):

Strict monotonicity This means that it should be compliant with the Pareto dominance relation from Equation 4.11:

$$\forall A, B \in \Psi : A \succ B \Rightarrow I(A) > I(B) \tag{4.12}$$

This definition guarantees that if set A dominates B then also the corresponding indicator value of A is greater than that of B.

Scaling invariance If the objective function values are scaled by monotonic transformation, e.g. normalizing them to $[0,1]$, the value of I must not change.

Efficient computation It should be cheap to compute the measure I.

Whereas the first property is essential, the last two are simply "nice to have".

Quite a lot of different ways to assess the quality of Pareto set approximations exist, such as the R indicator family, the Epsilon Indicator family, or the hypervolume indicator (see [71] and [38] for more thorough overviews). Especially the latter is quite commonly used, since it is currently the only indicator that is strictly monotonic. The concept of the hypervolume indicator is quite simple. As the name already suggest, it computes the hypervolume enclosed by the solutions in the Pareto set approximation. However, this requires the choice of a point from which the hypervolume is spanned. Ideally, such a reference point has objective values that are worse than any value from any solution in the set. Figure 4.7 shows the hypervolume for a Pareto set (with two objective functions). The hypervolume is computed by taking

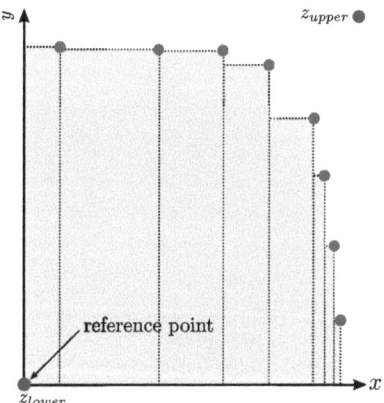

Figure 4.7: Hypervolume enclosed by a Pareto set.

the union of all hypercubes, which are constructed from the reference point and one of the solutions as the opposite corners. In the two-dimensional case this is quite simple. However in the general case, hypervolume computation requires runtime exponential in the number of objectives [9]. Therefore the hypervolume is usually approximated in higher dimensional optimization problems. However, for two objectives computation is easy as the hypervolume area can be split into several non-overlapping rectangles whose area can be summed up, as indicated in Figure 4.7.

In principle the hypervolume can be computed for any set of feasible solutions, not only for non-dominated solutions. Consequently, the hypervolume is defined for any arbitrary set

$A \in \Omega$ where $\Omega = 2^S$ is the set of all feasible solutions. Then

$$I_H(A) := \int_{\boldsymbol{z}_{lower}}^{\boldsymbol{z}_{upper}} \alpha_A(\boldsymbol{z}) d\boldsymbol{z} \tag{4.13}$$

where α_A is the so-called *attainment function*

$$\alpha_A(\boldsymbol{z}) = \begin{cases} 1 & : \ A \succ \{z\} \\ 0 & : \ \text{otherwise} \end{cases} \tag{4.14}$$

It returns 1 for all points that are dominated by any point in A, and otherwise returns 0. The integral's lower boundary $\boldsymbol{z}_{lower}$ corresponds to the reference point, whereas the upper boundary $\boldsymbol{z}_{upper}$ must be chosen to be any point that is not dominated by A (e.g. the utopian optimal solution, see Figure 4.7). The choice of the reference point has a huge effect on I_H whereas the upper boundary does not change the value (as long it is a non-dominated point) because there are no dominated points outside A.

Using I_H allows for a quantitative comparison of several Pareto set approximations even in cases when they are incomparable with the Pareto dominance relation.

4.4.3 Solving multi-objective optimization problems

Since many real-world optimization problems are multi-objective there exists a huge collection of methods and algorithms for solving them, see e.g. [51] or [16] for overviews. Some of the approaches, called *no-preference methods*, seek to find only a single solution in cases where the user is satisfied with any Pareto optimal solution. We shall not discuss them any further, since in practical applications of MSDS the user would like to have a selection of solutions, from which he can choose (maybe based on some other constraints). The remaining approaches can be roughly grouped into *a-priori* and *a-posteriori* methods. Whereas the latter automatically find a set of solutions, from which the user can choose, the former usually find only a single solution based on the preferences for certain objectives that the user must articulate beforehand. However, some a-priori methods can be converted into an a-posteriori method by systematically varying the parameters the user would normally define.

Popular a-priori methods comprise:

Lexicographic ordering The objectives are ordered by the user and the most important objective is optimized first. If a single solution exists, then this is the optimal solution, otherwise the second objective is optimized with the first objective's value as a constraint. The process continues until either a single solution is found or all objectives have been optimized. In practice it is hard to determine if only a single solution exists. Additionally, by ordering the objectives, the user can only articulate very rough preferences since the first objective is infinitely more important than the second.

Goal programming The user has to set "aspiration levels" z_i for each objective that should be reached. These can e.g. be minimal values for each objective function. The constraints

$f_i(\boldsymbol{x}) \geq z_i$ are called the goals, i.e. the function values should at least be as high as the aspiration levels. Of course, not all objectives can be maximized to the chosen aspiration levels and the differences $\theta_i = \max(0, z_i - f_i(\boldsymbol{x}))$ between attained function values are called the deviations. Goal programming then tries to minimize the weighted sum of the deviations whereby at the same time using the goals as side constraints.

$$\text{Minimize} \quad \sum_{i=1}^{n} w_i \theta_i$$
$$\text{Subject to} \quad f_j(\boldsymbol{x}) + \theta_i \geq z_i \quad \text{for all } j = 1...n$$
$$\theta_i \geq 0 \quad \text{for all } j = 1...n$$

Goal programming is a common method for multi-objective optimization problems since setting the aspiration levels is quite easy for the user. This is not the case for the weights, since they do not necessarily have an understandable interpretation in the original problem. Also the automated conversion into an a-posteriori method is not straightforward since the aspiration levels are problem dependent.

In practice it is often complicated to set goals beforehand, because, for example, objective function values are too abstract (e.g. diversity). Also a strict ordering is quite often undesirable. Therefore a-posteriori methods are usually preferred, because they present the user a set of solutions from which he can pick one or more, even based on additional criteria that have not been used in the optimization process. Some commonly used a-posteriori methods include:

Weighting method All objective functions are linearly combined into a single function by assigning weights to each objective: Maximize $\sum_{i=1}^{n} w_i f_i(\boldsymbol{x})$. This approach is simple and can easily be automated by sampling the w_i between 0 and 1. One drawback of the weighting approach is that it cannot find solutions in non-convex regions of the Pareto front [19]. The Pareto front is said to be convex if the line between any pair of points of the front is completely inside the feasible region. This is illustrated (for the two-dimensional case) in Figure 4.8. The Pareto front in the left diagram is convex whereas in the right figure it is non-convex because of the "hollow" in the middle of the front. Solutions Q and R cannot be connected by a straight line running inside the feasible area. This prevents solution P from being found by the weighting method. The two weighting coefficients define the slope of tangents on the Pareto front. In order to find the maximum value, the tangent is moved as near to the right upper corner (the utopian point) as possible, such that it is still a tangent on the front. However, the shown tangent in P (and in fact any tangent in P) intersects the Pareto front also in point Q. This means the tangent can be moved perpendicularly to itself to reach points on the Pareto front that have a higher sum value for the same weights, such as T in the example.

Non-convexity can be a problem in practice but in all applications discussed here the space is either convex or has only very small/few non-convex regions that are negligible (see the chapter about experiments). By systematically varying the weights a set of solutions

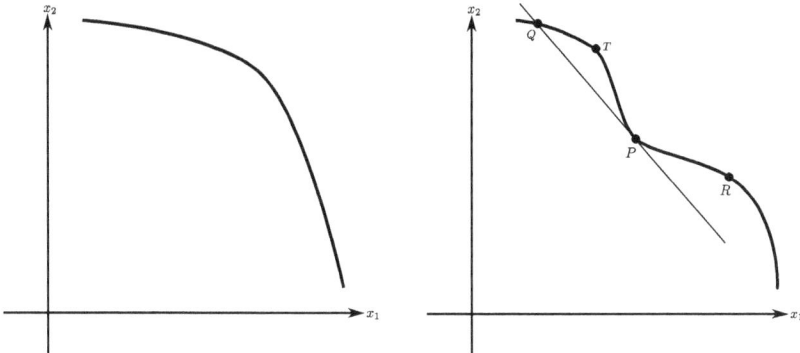

Figure 4.8: Convex (left) and non-convex (right) Pareto fronts. Solution P on the right front cannot be found by a linear combination of both objectives.

is gradually constructed. However, the number of different weight combinations grows exponentially with the number of variables, therefore this approach is only feasible for few variables.

ϵ-constraint method Only one objective function is optimized, the remaining are converted into constraints:

$$\text{Maximize} \quad f_l(\boldsymbol{x})$$
$$\text{Subject to} \quad f_j(\boldsymbol{x}) \geq \epsilon_j \quad \text{for all } j \in \{1, ..., n\} - \{l\}$$

In contrast to the weighting approach, the method does not require the solution space to be convex. However, the ϵ_j must be carefully chosen such that the whole system does not become infeasible, which requires a preliminary analysis of the problem.

Value function method The user needs to define a scalar so-called *value function*:

$$\text{Maximize} \quad v(\boldsymbol{f}(\boldsymbol{x}))$$

This is the more general case of the weighting method. In practice it is quite hard if not impossible to define a suitable value function.

Method of weighted metrics This method resembles the weighting approach, but instead of directly optimizing the weighted objective functions, they are first set in relation to the *ideal objective vector* $\boldsymbol{z}^*$, which consists of each objective's individual optimal value, and then a metric is applied:

$$\text{Minimize} \quad \left(\sum_{i=1}^{n} w_i \left(z_i^* - f_i(\boldsymbol{x}) \right)^k \right)^{1/k}$$

The usage of a metric emphasizes the greatest deviation with increasing k. E.g. using

$k = 1$ leads to the weighting approach (except for the constant $\boldsymbol{z}^*$), $k = 2$ is the methods of least squares, and for $k \to \infty$ only the greatest deviation is minimized.

When using this method, the same problem arises as is incurred via the weighting approach: the problem must be convex in order to find all Pareto optimal solutions. For this reason, a different form, known as the *weighted Chebyshev problem*, is often used:

$$\text{Minimize} \max_{1 \leq i \leq n} \left(w_i |f_i(\boldsymbol{x}) - z_i^*| \right)$$

If additionally $\boldsymbol{z}^*$ is set to the utopian solution vector (i.e. better than any Pareto optimal solution), finding all Pareto optimal solutions is guaranteed.

Achievement scalarizing function approach This method is very similar to the weighted Chebyshev problem, except that the the absolute value is dropped. It enables any reference point $\boldsymbol{z}$ to be used.

$$\text{Minimize} \max_{1 \leq i \leq n} \left(w_i (z_i - f_i(\boldsymbol{x})) \right)$$

Coming back to MSDS the question arises as to which method should be used for MSDS. The next section discusses the approach we have chosen for solving MSDS with existing single-objective algorithms.

4.5 Turning MSDS into a single-objective problem

As we will see later in Chapter 6, there are several heuristics for solving diversity selection problems. However, they have no knowledge about the objects' scores. Therefore the scores have to be integrated into the distances. This can be achieved by adding the scores of both objects to each distance (this is equivalent to adding the node labels to the labels of the adjacent edges).

$$d'(u_i, u_j) := d(u_i, u_j) + \sigma(u_i) + \sigma(u_j) \tag{4.15}$$

This transformation can be thought of as a deformation of the original space that (after normalization) stretches distances between highly scored objects and shrinks them between low scored objects. Therefore heuristics that work only on the distance matrix can be used to solve this modified problem. However, so far they produce only a single solution, but the goal is to present the user a set of solutions as produced by multi-objective genetic algorithms. This is where the weighting method presented above comes into play. The scalarized objective function of MSDS can be written as (see also Section 4.3)

$$f(S) = \alpha \sum_{i=1}^{p} \sigma(u_i) + (1 - \alpha)\delta(S) \quad , u_i \in S \tag{4.16}$$

If we choose δ_{ds} as diversity function, then Equation 4.16 becomes

$$f(S) = \alpha \sum_{i=1}^{p} \sigma(u_i) + (1-\alpha) \sum_{i=1}^{p} \sum_{j=1}^{p} d(u_i, u_j) \qquad (4.17)$$

Note that each distance is counted twice and thus the diversity objective is about twice as large as usual. This can easily be compensated for by different values for α. Further transformations yield

$$f(S) = \alpha \sum_{i=1}^{p} \sigma(u_i) + (1-\alpha) \sum_{i=1}^{p} \sum_{j=1}^{p} d(u_i, u_j) \qquad (4.18)$$

$$= \sum_{i=1}^{p} \left(\alpha \sigma(u_i) + \sum_{j=1}^{p} (1-\alpha) d(u_i, u_j) \right) \qquad (4.19)$$

$$= \sum_{i=1}^{p} \sum_{j=1}^{p} \alpha \frac{\sigma(u_i)}{p} + (1-\alpha) d(u_i u_j) \qquad (4.20)$$

$$= \sum_{i=1}^{p} \sum_{j=1}^{p} \alpha \frac{\sigma(u_i) + \sigma(u_j)}{2p} + (1-\alpha) d(u_i, u_j) \qquad (4.21)$$

$$= \sum_{i=1}^{p} \sum_{j=1}^{p} d''(u_i, u_j) \qquad (4.22)$$

with $d''(u_i, u_j) = \dfrac{\alpha}{2p} (\sigma(u_i) + \sigma(u_j)) + (1-\alpha) d(u_i, u_j) \qquad (4.23)$

Thus if each score $\sigma(u_i)$ value is divided by $2p$ then using the transformed distance d'' is essentially the same as using the weighting approach directly.

Unfortunately this only holds if p-dispersion-sum is the desired diversity measure. Applying the above distance transformation to either p-dispersion or p-center slightly different functions are optimized. For p-dispersion the weighted objective function is[1]

$$f(S) = \alpha \frac{\sum_{i=1}^{p} \sigma(u_i)}{p} + (1-\alpha) \min_{1 \leq i < j \leq p} d(u_i, u_j) \qquad (4.24)$$

whereas using the adapted distances d' yields

$$f(S) = \min_{1 \leq i < j \leq p} (\alpha(\sigma(u_i) + \sigma(u_j)) + (1-\alpha) d(u_i, u_j)) \qquad (4.25)$$

The same holds for p-center, where the weighting approach leads to

$$f(S) = \alpha \frac{\sum_{i=1}^{p} \sigma(u_i)}{p} + (1-\alpha)(1 - \max_{1 \leq i \leq n} \min_{1 \leq j \leq p, t \neq j} d(u_i, u_j)) \qquad (4.26)$$

---

[1] In this case it is advisable not to use the sum of scores as first objective but rather divide it by p such that the score objective has a comparable value range to the diversity objective, which is a single distance only in this case (still assuming that scores and distances are normalized).

whereas applying the transformation yields

$$f(S) = 1 - \max_{1 \leq i \leq n} \min_{1 \leq j \leq p, i \neq j} \left(\alpha(\sigma(u_i) + \sigma(u_j)) + (1-\alpha)d(u_i, u_j) \right) \quad (4.27)$$

Of course the fact that using the transformed edge labels alters the original optimization problems is not optimal. However, one has to keep in mind that all used algorithms are heuristics anyway (since the problem is $\mathcal{NP}$-hard) and there is no guarantee that they will find an optimal solution and they do not strictly optimize "the one" function they were originally applied to. In practice it turns out that the heuristics solutions are quite satisfactory. Still, using algorithms originally designed for single-objective problems with multiple objectives by applying some kind of transformation remains a compromise.

Another fact that needs to be checked, is if the above transformation still yields metric distances if the original distance is metric. This is crucial if the single-objective algorithms require metric distances in order to work properly or to guarantee a certain solution quality. Given that node labels are non-negative and the scaling parameter $\alpha \leq 1$:

$$d(x,y) \leq d(x,z) + d(z,y)$$
$$(1-\alpha)d(x,y) \leq (1-\alpha)d(x,z) + (1-\alpha)d(z,y)$$
$$\leq (1-\alpha)d(x,z) + (1-\alpha)d(z,y) + 2\alpha l(z)$$
$$\alpha(l(x) + l(y)) + (1-\alpha)d(x,y) \leq \alpha(l(x) + l(z)) + (1-\alpha)d(x,z)$$
$$+ \alpha(l(z) + l(y)) + (1-\alpha)d(z,y)$$

Therefore the triangle inequality still holds after incorporating the node labels into the edge labels.

Although for MSDS it was possible to find a transformation to a single-objective problem, this need not be the case for many other problems. Quite often a specific optimization algorithm for one or more objectives is not known or too inefficient because the (sub)problem itself is intractable such as the diversity objective of MSDS. Then none of the above approaches are of much help since they assume that either each single objective or the combined objective function can be optimized somehow. For single-objective problems the last resort, which in many cases works surprisingly well, are the so-called *metaheuristics* (see next chapter). Fortunately some metaheuristics can easily be adapted to work with multiple objectives without without having to fall back on any of the above mentioned approaches to weight, sort, or combine in any way the objective functions. Therefore the next chapter gives an introduction to metaheuristics in general and then focuses on evolutionary approaches, which are especially suited for multi-objective optimization problems.

Chapter 5

Metaheuristics for Optimization Problems

Metaheuristics are a class of several general algorithms for solving all kinds of optimization problems. Their popularity arises from the fact that they can be used even when little about the search space is known or it is hard to describe it in formal terms. The only thing that needs to be known about the problem, is a function for comparing (or ranking) possible solutions. This type of function usually exists, as what needs to be optimized should already be known. A metaheuristic then gradually changes one (or several) solutions and checks whether or not the new solution is better. These changes are of course problem dependent and a suitable internal representation of solutions is crucial for all approaches.

The algorithms mainly differ in the number of solutions that are processed (one or many), but also in how local optima are avoided and how new solutions are created based on existing one(s). On the one hand there are the so-called *trajectory methods*, which work with a single solution only. This solution is gradually changed and the search space is explored along a trajectory. Without any further modifications this search is directed towards the best solution in the neighborhood of the current solution. However, this approach easily gets held up in local optima. There are several methods that can be used to avoid this premature convergence, the most popular being simulated annealing and tabu search.

On the other hand there are *population based* methods, which maintain a set of solutions that are combined in a certain way to generate new and supposedly better solutions. Solutions can be combined based on their internal representation, e.g. in genetic algorithms, or a common "memory" of all solutions is used in order to guide the population towards the optimal solutions. The latter is performed for example in ant colony optimization or particle swarm optimization. Population based methods have a slight advantage over trajectory based methods in that by using several solutions at a time the search space can be explored more thoroughly and getting held up in local optima is less likely to happen. This of course comes with a considerably higher computational complexity.

It is easy to see that population based approaches are better suited for approximating a Pareto front when applied to multi-objective problems, since they generally work with a collection of solutions.

Since the focus of this thesis is not to find the best existing metaheuristic for MSDS, but rather to come up with algorithms that solve MSDS quickly and provide qualitatively acceptable solutions, we have only included metaheuristics as a reference to what can be achieved without in-depth studies of MSDS. Quite naturally the question arises, which metaheuristic to choose. Selection was simple, as in the MO community evolutionary algorithms and especially genetic algorithms are by far the most commonly used and best studied metaheuristic. The book from Coello et al. [16] is one of best sources on multi-objective evolutionary algorithm and it also contains a discussion about how other metaheuristics can be adopted to multiple objectives and information about their advantages and disadvantages. We repeat the most important facts here in order to further justify the decision for genetic algorithms.

Simulated Annealing Being a trajectory method considerable effort must be made to create a set of solutions. A crucial aspect of simulated annealing is the cooling strategy, which is often hard to find even in the single-objective case. In the multi-objective case additionally it has to account for diversity in the solution set, which renders it even more complicated. Although several multi-objective simulated annealing approaches exist, none of them has been shown to outperform evolutionary algorithms.

Tabu Search Similar to simulated annealing the algorithm needs considerable changes for creating a set of solutions. Maintaining diversity among the solutions is also a problem because tabu search usually modifies solutions so that its offspring are in the near neighborhood.

Ant Colony Optimization This metaheuristic implicitly maintains several solutions and thus is capable of finding several solutions with only minor modifications. Also no explicit means of maintaining a good spread of the solutions in the search space is needed. However, ant colony optimization requires an ordering on the objectives and usually fine tuning of quite a few parameters.

Particle Swarm Optimization Whereas this type of metaheuristic is easy to implement on the one hand – the algorithm works with multiple solutions (the particles) at the same time – it is quite hard to maintain diversity since in the single-objective case the particles should converge to one single solution.

Of course, the reported facts may not hold for all problems and MSDS might suit one of these heuristics especially well. But as already mentioned, it is out of the scope of this thesis to check every possible metaheuristic to see which works best.

The next sections begin with a general description of genetic algorithms. In Section 5.2 we discuss multi-objective genetic algorithms and present NSGA-II as one popular representative, which we have used for the various experiments. Due to the fact that as well as the ranking function, genetic algorithms need an abstract gene-like representation of solutions, as in the case of MSDS fixed-sized subsets, in Section 5.3 we finally present several genetic encoding of subsets, together with genetic operators.

5.1 Single-objective genetic algorithms

Genetic algorithms or the more general term evolutionary algorithms are, as their name suggests, inspired by evolution in nature. In short, evolution consists of two main parts: Mendelian inheritance [50], which explains how information is passed from one generation to the other, and Darwin's principle of natural selection [18].

All genetic information is encoded on the genome, which consists of several genes. Each gene can have different values, the so-called alleles. Formulated in more mathematical terms, each genome can be represented by a string or tuple of length n from some alphabet A:

$$g \in \mathcal{A}^n \tag{5.1}$$

The positions in the string are the genes, the values from the alphabet the alleles. Traditionally, in genetic algorithms $\mathcal{A} = \{0, 1\}$, i.e. genomes are represented as bit strings, but also integer based alphabets are commonly used. In humans the alleles are formed by the four bases adenine, cytosine, guanine and thymine, i.e. $\mathcal{A} = \{A, C, G, T\}$.

Inheritance, in a very simplified version, is the combination of two genomes (in the sexual case), usually by *crossover*. This means that two genomes are split at a certain position and the new offspring genome consists of the first part of the first parent genome, and the second part of the second parent genome, see Figure 5.1 (actually, two offspring are created, the second consisting of the first part of the second parent, and the second part of the first parent). Besides this single-point crossover also two-, or, in general, m-point crossover is possible. A special case is uniform crossover, where every even gene comes from the first parent and every odd from the second. Nature dictates a second way for genomes to change, namely by way of *mutation*. Mutation randomly changes the structure of the genome, e.g. by exchanging the value of one gene with another of its alleles. This is depicted in Figure 5.2.

Figure 5.1: One-point crossover of two parent genomes

Figure 5.2: Mutation of a single gene

The second main principle behind evolution is natural selection, which is even simpler than inheritance (on an abstract level). Selection means that from a large pool of offspring only the ones that are best adapted to environmental conditions will survive and be given the chance to inherit their properties further to their offspring. This, however, indirectly implies that the *phenotypic* fitness of an individual to survive in nature is more or less completely encoded in its *genotype*, which is represented by the genome. Taking both, inheritance and selection, leads to constant evolution in which the individuals adapt more and more to their environment and can even indirectly respond to its changes.

Genetic algorithms adapt this concept of natural evolution to arbitrary optimization problems. An instance of a (possible) solution to the optimization problem has to be represented in a way compatible to Equation 5.1, which is accompanied by a set of crossover and mutation operators. This means, there has to be a mapping function

$$c : \mathcal{A} \mapsto \chi \tag{5.2}$$

that maps the internal genetic representation into the actual search space χ. This search space can be structured in any arbitrary way. An example are combinations $\binom{m}{p}$ (which are discussed in more detail in Section 5.3), where the abstract representation is a tuple of object indices, i.e. $\mathcal{A} = \{1, 2, ..., m\}$ and $n = p$. An example for a combination of $p = 4$ out of $m = 10$ possible objects is the 4-tuple $(1, 4, 5, 9)$. The order of elements is not important. However, the choice of representing combinations as n-tuples also illustrates the fact that not every element from $\mathcal{A}^n$ necessarily maps to an element in χ, i.e. there are genetic representations which are not valid solutions to the problem. The 4-tuple $(1, 1, 2, 3)$ is not a valid 4-combination, since element 1 occurs twice. Hence, the actual search space $\mathcal{S}$ is usually only a subset:

$$\mathcal{S} \subseteq \mathcal{A}^n \tag{5.3}$$

Therefore special care has to be taken when designing a genetic representation and corresponding genetic operators.

The main aspect is the simulation of the environment, which is usually done by a fitness function f that assigns each individual's genotype a value corresponding to its phenotype's quality:

$$f : \mathcal{S} \mapsto \mathbb{R} \tag{5.4}$$

By convention smaller values of f mean better solutions, i.e. genetic algorithms perform a minimization. It could be, for example, the difference between the current function value and the desired function value (if it is known). Finally the selection process is mimicked, based on the fitness values. This can be done by e.g. giving better individuals a higher chance for reproduction and/or survival than less optimal individuals. Several selection schemes are commonly used, such as

- roulette wheel selection, where the probability of an individual being selected is proportional to its fitness,

- rank-based selection, where the selection probability is proportional to the individual's rank (this avoids premature convergence, such as in roulette wheel selection, if some individuals are much fitter than the rest of the population), or

- tournament selection, where a small set of individuals is randomly drawn and the one that has the best fitness wins the tournament and is selected.

The process of selection, reproduction, and fitness evaluation is iteratively executed until some stopping criterion is met, which can be a fixed number of generations, when a satisfying solution has been found, or when no improvements are made any more. This general scheme of genetic algorithms is depicted in Figure 5.3.

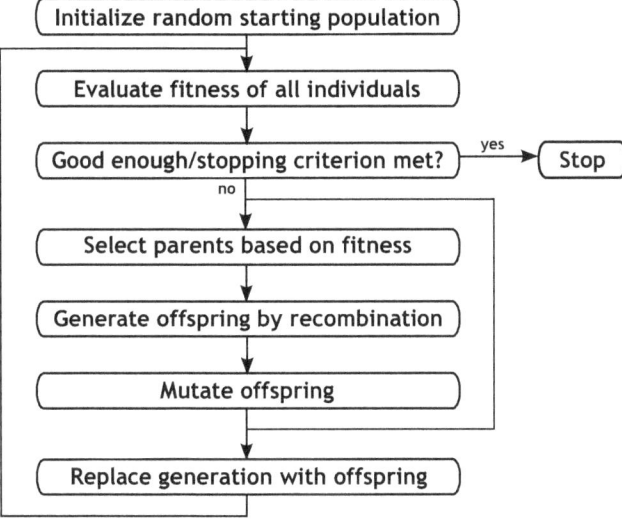

Figure 5.3: General scheme of a genetic algorithm

Fortunately, this general scheme is not only applicable for single-objective problems but also works for multiple objectives. Nevertheless some modifications are necessary, which are described in the following section.

5.2 Multi-objective genetic algorithms

As we have just seen, one main component of genetic algorithms is the fitness function that assigns each individual a single fitness values, which is later on used for selection. However in Chapter 4 we have seen that when dealing with multi-objective problems, no single quality criterion exists and solutions cannot be ranked in a total order. Nevertheless, fitness functions still exist, but each objective has its own, as in the single-objective case. There are two types of multi-objective genetic algorithms that can be distinguished by the way they use the different fitness functions to rank individuals. One class uses the dominance relation, whereas the other takes some indicator function (see Section 4.4). Fortunately, all other ingredients of genetic algorithms – genetic representations, operators, selection strategies – can be used unmodified for multi-objective problems. Dominance-based algorithms are by far the most widely used. The main reason is that they are usually faster than indicator-based ones, since many indicators cannot be computed efficiently. The reason why there is a need for a second algorithm class at all, is the fact that the dominance relation rapidly loses significance if the number of objectives increases. The more objectives are involved, the more likely it is for a single solution to be non-dominated in at least one objective. This can be circumvented by directly optimizing the chosen indicator function, e.g. the hypervolume indicator. However, since MSDS is a problem with only two objectives, there is no need to resort to more complicated indicator based algorithms and thus we shall not discuss them further.

Dominance-based algorithms use multiple fitness functions to establish the non-dominated relation between pairs of individuals. Intuitively, non-dominated individuals are fitter than dominated ones and should be preferred during combination. Still, it is unclear how two mutually non-dominated solutions are to be compared. Here another aspect of multi-objective optimization comes into play, namely the diversity of the non-dominated set. Unfortunately, multi-objective genetic algorithms face a similar problem to MSDS: getting as near to the real Pareto front as possible (=finding solutions of maximum score) while at the same time covering the complete front as well as possible (=selecting a diverse set of solutions on the front). Therefore the second ranking criterion in almost all multi-objective genetic algorithms deals with maintaining a good diversity in the population. The exact way in which this is achieved is the main aspect in which all dominance-based algorithms, such as NPGA[34], SPEA2[72], or NSGA-II[21] differ from each other.

NPGA

NPGA (Niched Pareto Genetic Algorithm) was one of the first algorithms to be successfully applied to multi-objective problems. Selection is carried out in two steps. First two individuals are randomly chosen to take part in a tournament. However, instead of making a direct one-to-one comparison, a second comparison set is drawn from the population. Each of the two candidates is then compared against each individual in the set. If one dominates the set and the other does not, it wins the tournament and is selected. If this first round ends without a winner (both are dominating the set or none does), the tie is broken by applying niching techniques which are also used in single-objective GAs (see [45] for an extensive overview). Niching tries to avoid the whole population crowing around one (local) optimum but instead maintains several sub-populations around other (local) optima. One popular way is *fitness sharing* where individuals in the same niche share their fitness values. The more crowded the niche, the more the individual fitness values are decreased and some of the solutions in that region are then discarded because other, slightly less fit solutions, in other less crowded niches, have a higher value after fitness sharing. Sharing is performed by defining a niche sharing radius $\sigma_{sharing}$, counting the number of neighbors (measured in either genotype or phenotype space) inside the radius and then degrading the raw fitness in proportion to the niche count. Since in the multi-objective case there is no single fitness value, NPGA only uses the niche count itself: individuals with less neighbors are preferred. Presumably for performance reasons, the niche count is only computed in the comparison set and not the whole population. The complete selection process is depicted in Figure 5.4. Both marked candidates i and j neither dominate the comparison set nor are they completely dominated. Therefore the number of individuals inside the two niches, defined by $\sigma_{sharing}$, decides that individual i wins.

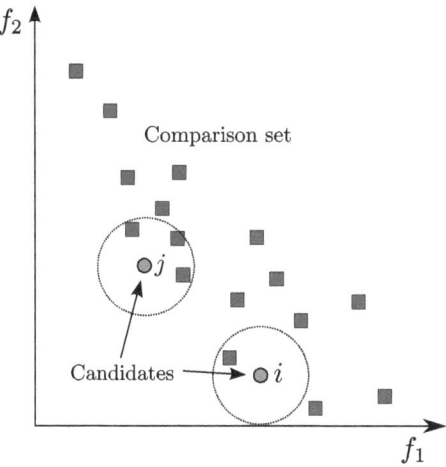

Figure 5.4: Ranking by dominance and niche count performed by NPGA.

The major drawback of NPGA is its lack of an elitism strategy i.e. the best individuals are not necessarily carried over into the next generation. It has been shown that elitism improves convergence considerably and therefore NPGA is outperformed by more recent algorithms such as SPEA2 or NSGA-II.

SPEA2

In contrast to NPGA, SPEA uses a so-called archive – in addition to the regular population – in which the best individuals are permanently stored and carried on into future generations. The algorithm starts with an empty archive and a randomly generated population. Then fitness values are calculated for all individuals, both in the population and the archive (which is non-empty after the first iteration). Fitness values are computed based on the so-called strength values, which are the numbers of individuals dominated by a solution. Non-dominated solutions have a strength value of 0. Then for each solution the strength values of all dominating solutions are summed up to form the raw fitness value. Figure 5.5 show a sample population together with the strength and raw fitness values.

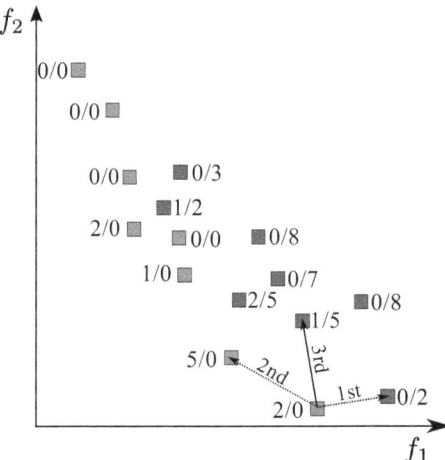

Figure 5.5: Fitness assignment in SPEA2. The first value beneath the solutions indicates the strength value, whereas the second value indicates raw fitness. Non-dominated solutions (in green) always have raw fitness values of zero. An example for the density computation is shown for $k = 3$.

In order to distinguish between individuals with the same raw fitness value, a density value is computed for each solution. It is computed by taking the inverse of the distance to the k-th nearest neighbor, which is usually chosen to be the square root of the size of both the population and the archive. This ensures that individuals in sparsely populated regions are favored (both raw fitness and density values are to be minimized). After fitness assignment all non-dominated individuals (from both the population and the previous archive) are copied to the new archive. If the archive is not completely filled up dominated solutions are added according to their raw fitness and density values. If the archive is overfilled solutions are removed based on their density values. The individual with the smallest distance to its k-th nearest neighbor is iteratively removed until the archive has the desired size. Finally binary tournament selection is performed on the archive (not on the population!) and mutation and combination operators are applied to shape the population for the next generation.

While SPEA2, with sophisticated fitness assignment and archive management procedures, has advantages over NSGA-II, when it comes to many objectives it is more complicated to implement. Since MSDS involves two objectives only, we have chosen the simpler NSGA-II algorithm.

NSGA-II

Similar to most other dominance-based approaches, the algorithm uses the non-dominated relation between all solutions. First all globally non-dominated solutions are selected, put into the first so-called *front*, and temporarily removed from the population. After removal, another set of individuals exists that is now not dominated by any other remaining individual. They are selected again, put into the second front, and removed. This process is termed non-dominated sorting and continues until all solutions have been assigned to a front. The colors of the solutions shown in Figure 5.6 indicate the different fronts.

The index of the front is now used as a rank when it comes to selecting individuals for crossover. However, the rank is again not the only quality measure. Additionally the so-called *crowding distance* of each individual is taken into account. For this, the distances to its next neighbors along all objective axes are computed. They span a cuboid in which no other solutions reside, see Figure 5.6. For easier comparison and computation, the average length of all edges is taken as the crowding distance.

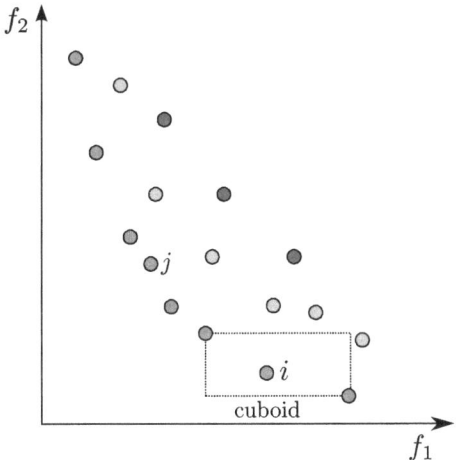

Figure 5.6: Computation of the crowding distance of individual i. The colors of the points indicate the different fronts they have been assigned to.

When it comes to selection, first the individuals' ranks are taken into account. If two individuals are in the same front their crowding distance is used to break ties, favoring individuals with larger crowding distances. Individual i in the figure has a greater crowding distance than j and would therefore be preferred. This ensures that the algorithm spreads the solutions more uniformly over the Pareto front and does not get trapped in local optima too early. These two criteria define a partial order $\geq_{cd}$ on all solutions:

$$i \geq_{cd} j \Leftrightarrow (rank(i) < rank(j)) \vee ((rank(i) = rank(j)) \wedge (cdist(i) > cdist(j)))$$

Differing from the original NSGA-II algorithm, which works with standard binary tournament selection, unbiased tournament selection[63] was used for the experiments instead. This approach reduces the variance in the probability of an individual getting selected for a tournament. This cased the loss of diversity in the next generation (because certain individuals are never picked for a tournament) to be reduced. Algorithm 1 shows NSGA-II's main function. The key functions – non-dominated sorting and crowding distance assignment – are shown in algorithms 2 and 3, respectively.

Algorithm 1: NSGA-II
---
1 $P_0 \leftarrow$ random initial population;
2 $t \leftarrow 0$;
3 **while** *not finished* **do**
4     $T_t \leftarrow P_t \cup C_t$;
5     $F \leftarrow$ non-dominated-sort(T_t);
6     $i \leftarrow 0$;
7   **while** $|C_{t+1}| \leq N$ **do**
8   assign-crowding-distance(F_i);
9        $C_{t+1} \leftarrow C_{t+1} \cup F_i$;
10       $i \leftarrow i + 1$;
11   **end**
12   sort$(C_{t+1}, \geq_{cd})$;
13   $C_{t+1} \leftarrow C_{t+1}[0..N]$;
14   $C_{t+1} \leftarrow$ new-population(C_{t+1}); /* selection, crossover, mutation */
15   $t \leftarrow t + 1$;
16 **end**

Now that we have an algorithm that can optimize multi-objective problems the last thing that is missing in order to solve MSDS is a suitable genetic representation for the subsets. In the next section several possibilities, together with their genetic operators are presented.

5.3 Genetic representations and operators for subsets

The selection of a fixed number p of molecules from the whole dataset with m molecules is, in mathematical terms, a combination $\binom{m}{p}$. Since the term "combination" is already used in the GA community for combining two individuals by crossover, we shall use the term "subset" in the remainder of this chapter. In principle, such a subset can be represented and implemented as an unordered set in the genetic algorithm (e.g. a hash set) so that genotype and phenotype are identical. However, this poses several problems. Most importantly the notion of crossover between two individuals with one or more crossover points cannot be easily transferred to such a set representation. Therefore, it is favorable to implement subsets as ordered tuples or arrays on which crossover can be defined properly. Until recently only a single publication has described the optimization of subsets in genetic algorithms, together with one representation and corresponding operators [15]. Interestingly, for the other combinatorial concept of *permutations*, quite a number of publications on genetic representations have been published (see [41]

Algorithm 2: non-dominated-sort

Input : An intermediate population P
Output: A list of fronts F

/* S_i is the set of individuals that are dominated by i */
/* n_i is the number of individuals that dominate i */

1 **foreach** $p \in P$ **do**
2   **foreach** $q \in P$ **do**
3   **if** $p \succ q$ **then** $S_p \leftarrow S_p \cup \{q\}$;
4   **else if** $q \succ p$ **then** $n_p \leftarrow n_p + 1$;
5   **end**
6   **if** $n_p = 0$ **then** $F_1 \leftarrow F_1 \cup \{p\}$;
7 **end**
8 $i \leftarrow 1$;
9 **while** $F_i \neq \emptyset$ **do**
10    $T = \emptyset$;
11   **foreach** $p \in F_i$ **do**
12   **foreach** $q \in S_p$ **do**
13        $n_q \leftarrow n_q - 1$;
14   **if** $n_q = 0$ **then** $T \leftarrow T \cup \{q\}$;
15   **end**
16   **end**
17    $i \leftarrow i + 1$;
18    $F_i \leftarrow T$;
19 **end**
20 **return** F

Algorithm 3: assign-crowding-distance

Input: An intermediate population P

1 $l \leftarrow |P|$;
2 **foreach** $p \in P$ **do** $p_{dist} \leftarrow 0$; /* Initialize crowding distances   */
3 **foreach** *objective* m **do**
4    $P \leftarrow \text{sort}(P, m)$; /* Sort by m-th objective value   */
5    $P[0]_{dist} \leftarrow \infty$;
6    $P[l]_{dist} \leftarrow \infty$;
7   **for** $i \leftarrow 2..(l-1)$ **do**
      /* $P[i].m$ is the m-th objective value of $P[i]$ */
8      $P[i]_{dist} \leftarrow P[i]_{dist} + (P[i+1].m - P[i-1].m)$;
9   **end**
10 **end**

for an overview). Therefore during this thesis alternatives have been developed [49], which are described below.

5.3.1 Binary subset genomes and SX-crossover

In the mentioned published article, the p elements of a subset are encoded in a bit string of length m and if element i is selected, the bit at position i is set. For example, the bit string 010110 represents a subset "3 out of 6" and the selected elements are 2, 4 and 5 (if counted from left). The number of set bits must always be equal to p – the number of selected elements. The binary encoding automatically prevents one object being selected twice. However, genetic operators need to ensure that the number of set bits remains exactly p after their application.

In the original paper, Chen and Hou used the so-called exchange mutation operator. However, this is not particularly effective, as it randomly selects two elements (bits) and exchanges their values. Only in cases where $p \approx \frac{n}{2}$ does this really change the chromosome. In other cases the probability that two genes with different values are selected is rather low. This can, of course, be leveled out by increasing the mutation rate but then this depends on the settings of p and n. Therefore it is advisable to change the operator slightly so that it selects two random bits *with opposite values* and swaps them. This ensures that the genome changes in any case.

Crossover is more complicated, because usual crossover operators such as single-point, two-point, or uniform crossover would produce genomes with more or less than p set bits if the exchanged parts in the two parents do not contain the same number of 1s. Therefore the authors proposed a modified two-point crossover – called SX (shrinking crossover) – where first two random points are selected and one of the points is shifted towards the other until the region between the two points contains the same number of 1s in both parent genomes. Then the bits in this interval are mutually exchanged. This process is illustrated in Figure 5.7.

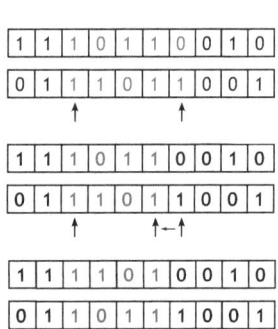

Figure 5.7: Shrinking crossover

5.3.2 Integer subset genomes with two-point crossover

Besides bit string representations a combination can easily be encoded in an integer array of length p that contains the selected objects' numbers. The same combination as above is then represented as [2,4,5]. This representation not only allows for easier access to the selected elements (in a bit string, the set bits need to be searched for). Additionally, combinations *with repetitions* can easily be evolved with only minor modifications to the operators, whereas with binary representation this becomes much more complicated (for our application, combinations without repetitions are sufficient). The fixed-sized array also ensures that a chromosome always consists of p selected elements, but special care has to be taken that no element appears twice.

Let us first discuss the mutation operator. In principle it works by selecting a random element j in the integer array and a random number $r < n$ and replacing j with r. However, this may lead to duplicate elements appearing in the array if r has already been selected before. Therefore, the complete array has to be checked for the existence of r and if so, new j and r are chosen and the process is repeated. Since mutation is usually only carried out on a small fraction of individuals this potentially time-consuming process is negligible.

The crossover operator works similarly to normal two-point crossover, however, again, special care has to be taken to ensure that no duplicate entries appear in the two arrays. First, two random points are selected and for the two offspring the numbers in between the two points are taken. The remaining entries are filled up with elements from the other individual *but only if a number has not yet been selected for the individual*. This can be checked by maintaining a bit set of selected elements. Entries still missing after this second step are consecutively filled up from the other individual – they are even taken from the middle interval. This operation is illustrated in Figure 5.8 for one of the offspring.

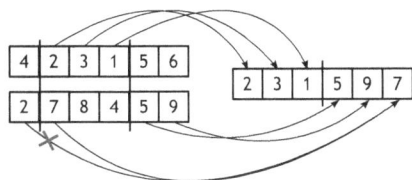

Figure 5.8: Two-point crossover for integer representations of combinations needs to be modified so that no duplicates appear in the offspring.

5.3.3 Integer subset genomes with uniform crossover

For some problems, such as our problem of diversity selection, uniform crossover works more efficiently or at least offers faster convergence. Therefore we have also implemented an adaption of uniform crossover for combinations in the integer array representation. For reasons of efficiency we decided to work with sorted arrays this time, as this makes it very easy to detect duplicate entries. Of course, the sorted order needs to be maintained throughout all operations. Therefore, the mutation operator is modified slightly. Instead of scanning the whole array for the new number r, this can be accomplished more easily in logarithmic time with binary search. If no duplicate is found, r needs to be inserted at the right position in order to keep the array sorted. This position can be determined quickly, because the binary search not only provides information about whether the element already exists, but also on its potential position in the array. The elements between the removed number and the insertion position of r are shifted accordingly and r is inserted at the free place. Figure 5.9 demonstrates this process with a small example. Implementing pseudo-uniform crossover with a sorted array is now straightforward. In principle every second element is exchanged between the two parent individuals, but again, this may introduce duplicate entries. However, using the two sorted arrays of both

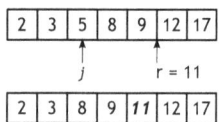

Figure 5.9: Mutation on integer representations works by selecting a random element from the array, replacing it with a random number and then shifting it to its right position in order to keep the array sorted.

parent individuals makes it easy to create a sorted combined array of length $2p$ containing all numbers from both individuals. Note, that a number can appear twice at most in this new array. If that is the case, both occurrences are next to each other. The two offspring are now created by taking all odd elements for the first child and all even elements for the second. This is demonstrated in Figure 5.10. This process ensures that both offspring arrays stay sorted.

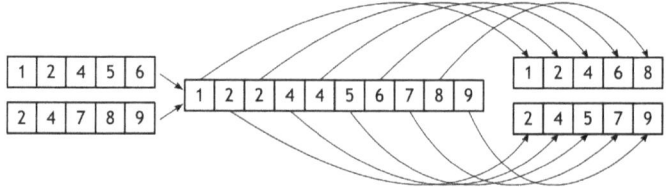

Figure 5.10: By using sorted arrays for the combination representation, uniform crossover can be performed easily.

5.3.4 Permutation-based subsets

As we shall see later in Chapter 7, the genetic algorithm has serious problems in approximating the whole Pareto front. While it is hard to determine the real cause of this problem, one effect is quite obvious when using the above-mentioned representations for combinations: Once an object is missing in all individuals – be it from the beginning or via several steps of recombination and selection – it is very hard to get it back into the population. Only mutation can introduce missing objects. This is different from most other genetic representations, such as permutations, in which the structure or order is important and in principle every possible solution can be created by recombination operators (at least it should be possible to do so). Therefore we also tested another type of genetic representations for combinations, which is based on permutations of all available objects. In order to interpret a permutation as a combination, a certain range of elements must be selected, e.g. the first p in the permutation. By using an encoding, where all objects are present at all times and the order determines which elements are in the corresponding combination, the above-mentioned problems of lost objects are avoided. Depending on the genetic operators applied to the permutations, a nice side-effect could be that important objects are successively moved to the front of the permutation. If the operators make only slight changes to the element order, positions at the front will prevent the elements from sliding out of the window that defines the combination. One potential drawback of the permutation-based representation is that quite a lot of work during recombination is performed that does not have an immediate effect on the combination. If the order of elements in the masked region is changed this does not influence the combination. It can, however, lead to significant changes in future generations. This can be seen as a kind of long-term memory, which may even turn out to be an advantage.

As already mentioned, a huge collection of genetic operators is available for permutations (see [41] for an overview). We have chosen two exemplary operators, the *PMX* [30] and *OX1* [20] operators. Of course, one should not infer from their behavior that all permutation operators behave similarly. However, if the above conjecture is right that the advantage of using a permutation's subsequence is that objects do not get lost, most operators should be able to exhibit this fact.

Both operators work on integer array representations where the position of the elements in the array is equal to their position in the permutation. The PMX (Partially-Mapped Crossover) operator tries to preserve absolute positions of objects from both parents. Consider two parent individuals

(1 2 3 4 5 6 7 8) and
(3 7 5 1 6 8 2 4)

(the examples are taken from [41]). First, similar to two-point crossover, two random cutting positions are chosen, e.g. between the third and fourth and between the sixth and seventh object:

(1 2 3 | 4 5 6 | 7 8)
(3 7 5 | 1 6 8 | 2 4)

The elements between the two crossover points define a mapping $4 \leftrightarrow 1$, $5 \leftrightarrow 6$, and $6 \leftrightarrow 8$. For the children, both mapping sections are used unaltered:

(. . . | 4 5 6 | . .)
(. . . | 1 6 8 | . .)

The missing positions are filled up with entries in the same position from the other parent, except if the number already exists in the child. For example, the 5 from the third position of the second parent is already present in the first child (in the mapping section). Therefore the mapping $5 \to 6$ is applied. In this case, 6 also already exist therefore the mapping $6 \to 8$ is used. Applying this scheme results in

(3 7 8 | 4 5 6 | 2 1)
(4 2 3 | 1 6 8 | 7 5)

It is easy to see that this operator is in principle able to (re-)add missing numbers into the combination-window. If, e.g., the window comprised the first four elements, then the 8 would be missing in both parent individuals. However, after applying the mapping it finally appears in the first children in third position.

The OX1 (Order Crossover, first version) operator explicitly makes use of the fact that for permutations only the order but not the actual position of elements is important. First it chooses two points in both parent individuals, similar to the PMX operator:

(1 2 3 | 4 5 6 | 7 8)
(3 7 5 | 1 6 8 | 2 4)

The parts between the crossover points are again copied unchanged into the children:

(. . . | 4 5 6 | . .)
(. . . | 1 6 8 | . .)

The missing entries are filled up starting at the second point (wrapping over to the start of the individual) in the order in which they appear in the other parent, also starting at the second cut point. That is, the first child is appended with 2. Then 4 is skipped since it is already present, then 3 and so on. The second child is constructed analogously:

(7 1 8 | 4 5 6 | 2 3)
(3 4 5 | 1 6 8 | 7 2)

It is quite obvious that any element can easily change its position and therefore fall out of or into the window.

There are other permutation operators, such as the CX-operator [55], that cannot prevent lost objects from never reappearing again because they only interchange numbers from equal positions in both parents (similar to uniform crossover for combinations). Unfortunately even the permutation-based operators cannot prevent inferior coverage of the Pareto front, as we shall demonstrate in Chapter 7. Therefore the usage of specialized heuristics, some of which are presented in the following chapter, becomes even more important.

Chapter 6

Heuristic Approaches

Even if metaheuristics work for almost any type of optimization problem, they are often not the best choice, especially if the problem structure is well understood and allows for problem-specific heuristics. They can benefit from the this background knowledge and allow for faster search and/or solutions of better quality. And as we shall see in the next chapter, one is usually well-advised to try other heuristics as well if possible.

Fortunately, since MSDS is similar to several graph-theoretic problems, some special heuristics have already been invented, such as Erkut's algorithms for the p-dispersion problem and Hochbaum&Shmoys' heuristic for the p-center problem. They are presented in the following two sections. Unfortunately both approaches only work on edge-labeled graphs and the node labels have to be incorporated somehow into the edge labels. How this can be achieved and its implications are discussed in Section 4.5. The third heuristic, which is the novel *Score Erosion* algorithm presented in Section 6.3, does not need such transformations and is also much faster than the former two.

6.1 Erkut's p-dispersion heuristic

In his paper on the p-dispersion problem [24], Erkut presented a heuristic approach for approximating diverse subsets. The problem is motivated by the placement of obnoxious facilities, such as nuclear power plants or missile silos. They should be placed as far apart from each other as possible in order to minimize collateral damage if one facility is destroyed. Although the presented algorithm has only been applied to the p-dispersion problem it can be used with only very little changed for p-dispersion-sum. The algorithm relies on the graph-based formulation of the diversity selection problem.

Starting with the complete set of all n nodes in the graph, nodes are iteratively deleted until only p remain. The decision, which nodes to remove, is based on a list of all edges in the graph, sorted ascendingly by their labels (i.e. distance). The shortest edge is removed from the list and one of its two nodes is deleted from the set. The choice, which of the two adjacent nodes is removed, is arbitrary and usually performed randomly. This has the advantage that several runs of the algorithms may result in different subsets enabling the user to pick the best one. The process of deleting nodes is repeated until only p nodes remain. This set is the starting point for the second phase, in which a local search is performed. Each node currently included in the solution set is exchanged with all currently unselected nodes, one at a time. If any such swap improves the objective function δ (either p-dispersion or p-dispersion-sum), it is accepted, otherwise it is rejected. Algorithm 4 shows this procedure in pseudo-code.

Algorithm 4: p-dispersion optimization heuristics

Input : A complete graph with edge labels G, the number of elements to select p
Output: A subset of objects optimizing the p-dispersion(-sum) measure

1 $E' \leftarrow E$ sorted ascendingly by labels;
2 Sel $\leftarrow V_G$;
3 **while** $|\text{Sel}| > k$ **do**
4      $\{u,v\} \leftarrow pop(E')$;
5   **if** $u \in$ Sel **then** Sel $\leftarrow$ Sel $- \{u\}$;
6   **else if** $v \in$ Sel **then** Sel $\leftarrow$ Sel $- \{v\}$;
7 **end**
8 **foreach** $u \in$ Sel **do**
9   **foreach** $v \in V_G -$ Sel **do**
10   Sel' $\leftarrow$ Sel $- \{u\} + \{v\}$;
11   **if** $\delta(\text{Sel}') > \delta(\text{Sel})$ **then** Sel $\leftarrow$ Sel';
12   **end**
13 **end**
14 **return** Sel

Both construction and local improvement take $O(n^2 \log n)$ time. In practice about half the time is usually spent in fully sorting the list of edges. This offers slight potential for improvement by e.g. using a heap, since usually only about half of the edges are needed. The runtime does not only depend on n; p also has a noticeable influence. For small p substantial time is spent sorting the list of edges, which requires $O(e \log e) = O(n^2 \log n)$ time. During the optimization step each currently selected node is interchanged with each non-selected node and the win (or loss) of this exchange has to be computed by looking at the weights of all adjacent edges. This leads to a complexity of $O(p(n-p)p) = O(p^2 n - p^3)$, and means that by increasing p the increase of runtime should slow down or even reverse.

The algorithm makes no guarantees about the solution quality. However, the experiments in Chapter 7 show that this simple heuristic performs surprisingly well for MSDS, both in combination with p-dispersion and p-dispersion-sum as diversity measures.

6.2 Hochbaum & Shmoys' p-center heuristic

Hochbaum and Shmoys were the first to present a best-possible heuristic for the p-center problem that runs in acceptable time [61]. The correctness proof of the approximation algorithm includes the two facts that the found solutions are at most twice as large as the optimal solution and that no other polynomial-time heuristic can guarantee a better approximation factor.

Even if the algorithm itself is barely more complicated than Erkut's, the reason why it finds an approximation to p-center is more difficult to see. In Section 3.2 we showed that the p-center problem is equivalent to finding a dominating set of size p in the graph. Therefore an algorithm that efficiently approximates the dominating set problem can also be used (with slight modifications) for p-center. The idea is the following: Instead of constructing a dominating set, an algorithm for finding a *maximal* independent set is used. This must not be confused with the *maximum* independent set, which is $\mathcal{NP}$-hard to determine and would therefore not be of great use. A maximal independent set denotes an independent set that cannot be extended further by additional nodes. However, there may exist other independent sets that are larger. Unfortunately, the size of a maximal independent set can be much larger than for a minimum dominating set in the same graph. This can be circumvented by the usage of the *square* G^2 of the graph G under consideration (ignoring the fact that we are dealing with complete graphs for now). The square of a graph G is the graph $G^2 = (V, E^2)$ with $E^2 = E \cup \{\{x_i, x_k\} | \{x_i, x_j\} \in E \wedge \{x_j, x_k\} \in E\}$. This means that G^2 contains all edges from G and additionally all connections between two nodes x_i and x_k if there is a path of length 2 between between these nodes. A maximal independent set in G^2 has a convenient property: it contains at most as many nodes as a minimum dominating set in G, therefore it can be used to approximate the latter.

The algorithm works on graphs G_i that only contain edges that are no longer than the i-th shortest edge. The key idea is to find the shortest edge length so that G_i^2 contains a maximal independent set of size not larger than p (and ideally equal to p). The edge e_i for which this condition is true then determines the value of the p-center measure: the nodes from the maximal independent set are the p centers, the minimal distances are exactly the edges in G_i and the longest such edge is e_i. It can further be proven that this construction yields a result that is at most twice as large as the optimal value.

Algorithm 5 uses a slight improvement in that it searches for the edge e_i by way of a binary search instead of a linear scan over all edges. The square of G_i is also not explicitly constructed but rather simulated by also looking at the neighbors' neighbors (see the two nested loops in the pseudo code).

The complexity of Hochbaum&Shmoys' heuristic is $O(|E|\log|E|)$ (which is equal to $O(n^2\log n)$ in complete graphs): The outer loop with the binary search runs $\log|E|$ times at most. Inside the loop each edge is examined once at most: if one of its two nodes is selected the edge is immediately deleted from G_i. Although the theoretical complexity of Hochbaum&Shmoys' algorithm is therefore equal to Erkut's heuristic in practice it runs much faster than the latter.

Practically speaking, runtime not only depends on the total number of nodes n but also on the number of selected nodes p, even if this is not obvious from the algorithm. The reason lies in the fact that with increasing p the *mid*-shortest edge gets much shorter (see lines 4,5 and 17,18 in algorithm 5). This leads to G_{mid} having fewer edges and thus fewer nodes are removed by the two innermost loops (lines 10–15) and more iterations are needed for the outer loop starting at line 8.

Algorithm 5: p-center optimization heuristics

Input : A complete graph with edge labels G, the number of elements to select p
Output: A subset of objects optimizing δ_c

1 low ← 1;
2 high ← $|V_G| * (|V_G| - 1)/2$;
3 **while** high >low +1 **do**
4   mid ← (high + low)/2;
5   G_{mid} ← G without edges longer than mid-shortest edge in G;
6   Sel ← ∅;
7   Avail ← V_G;
8   **foreach** $u \in$ Avail **do**
9   Sel ← Sel ∪ $\{u\}$;
10   **foreach** $\{u, v\} \in E_{G_{mid}}$ **do**
11   Avail ← Avail − $\{v\}$;
12   **foreach** $\{v, w\} \in E_{G_{mid}}$ **do**
13   Avail ← Avail − $\{w\}$;
14   **end**
15   **end**
16   **end**
17   **if** |Sel| $\leq p$ **then**
18   high ← mid;
19   Sel' ← Sel;
20   **else** low ← mid;
21 **end**
22 **return** Sel'

6.3 Score Erosion

The motivation for Score Erosion comes from its application in vHTS. The molecules are expected to exhibit so-called *neighborhood behavior* [58, 53]. This concept is similar to the structure activity relationship already mentioned in the introduction. Both describe the fact – or better the assumption – that molecules that are similar to each other show similar activities (SAR) or have similar properties (neighborhood behavior). As a graphic analogy, the term activity islands is often used, meaning that the molecular space contains mostly inactive molecules and only a few small islands with some active molecules exist. The height of these islands can be interpreted as the degree of activity. Using this analogy it becomes more clear what the problem with MSDS is: Huge high islands can shed the view of smaller and less high islands. Applying traditional vHTS methods, the molecules are sorted according to their scores and the usual approach would be to select the "top p" molecules. This very likely leads to finding only one, or at most, a few islands, and the diversity objective is completely ignored. Therefore, the idea is to select molecules step-by-step and reduce the score of all molecules u_i that are similar to the just selected molecule u_s by a certain amount after each step. This can be seen as an erosion of the current island which makes it shallower. This opens the chance for the less high islands to become more visible. The force of this erosion depends on the distance between u_i and u_s and a parameter β:

$$\sigma_{t+1}(u_i) = \left(1 - e^{-\frac{d(u_i, u_s)}{\beta}}\right) * \sigma_t(u_i) \tag{6.1}$$

The underlying assumption is that the islands are perfect Gauss bells where the highest peak is in the center of the islands and the heights (=scores) fall exponentially with increasing distance to the center. This assumption is somewhat idealistic and presumably will not appear in practice very often. It is however a sensible abstraction and actually works quite will. Algorithm 6 shows the pseudo-code for this approach.

Algorithm 6: Score Erosion

Input : A list with activities A, the complete distance matrix D, the number of objects to select p and the weighting parameter β

Output: A subset of objects that – depending on β – is a good trade-off between activity and diversity

1 Sel $= \emptyset$;
2 best $\leftarrow \max_p A[k]$;
3 **for** $i \leftarrow 1$ **to** p **do**
4   Sel $\leftarrow$ Sel $\cup$ {best};
5      $A[\text{best}] = -\infty$;
6   best$'$ = best;
7   **for** $j \leftarrow 1$ **to** n **do**
8          $A[j] \leftarrow A[j] * (1 - e^{-\frac{D[\text{best}, j]}{\beta}})$;
9   **if** $A[j] > A[\text{best}']$ **then** best$' \leftarrow j$;
10   **end**
11   best $\leftarrow$ best$'$;
12 **end**
13 **return** Sel

First, the highest ranked molecule is selected. Next the distance to all remaining molecules is computed and the scores of all molecules are decreased in proportion to the distance. The user-defined factor β controls how much the score is eroded. Using a large value for β decreases the scores of similar molecules quite extensively, therefore the diversity objective is favored, whereas a small β focuses more on the score objective. After the erosion step, the molecules are re-ranked based on the changed score values. These operations are iteratively performed until p elements have been selected.

The computation complexity of Score Erosion is $O(pn)$, since all the scores of all n molecules are decreased in each iteration and there are exactly p iterations. Therefore Score Erosion has a much lower theoretical complexity than both Erkut's and Hochbaum&Shmoys' heuristic. This becomes significant if the number of objects increases and becomes apparent in the experiments.

A very similar algorithm to Score Erosion was published in [69] in the context of pattern mining. The authors discuss the problem of extracting frequent patterns from a dataset that are significant on the one hand and have a low redundancy on the other (comparable to score and diversity in our application). The greedy algorithm they developed uses a similar update formula to Equation 6.1 but instead of multiplying the old value with the redundancy value to the selected pattern, they subtract it from the significance value:

$$\sigma_{t+1}(u_i) = \sigma_t(u_i) - \beta * d(u_i, u_s) \tag{6.2}$$

At first glance, this seems a bit odd, since significance and redundancy (or activity and distance) are two different concepts and subtracting one from the other does not have such an intuitive interpretation as the exponential erosion of the islands. The scores can even easily become negative, which, however is not a problem for the functionality of the algorithm. However, we also tried this update rule in the experiments and, as we shall see in the next chapter, it appears to work quite well for our application.

Since the idea behind Score Erosion is derived from a practical application, it is interesting to see which functions it optimizes:

$$f(S) = \sum_{i=1}^{p} \left(\sigma(u_i) - \beta \sum_{j=1}^{i-1} (1 - d(u_i, u_j)) \right) \quad \text{for the difference update rule} \tag{6.3}$$

$$f(S) = \sum_{i=1}^{p} \sigma(u_i) \prod_{j=1}^{i-1} \left(1 - e^{-\frac{d(u_i, u_j)}{\beta}} \right) \quad \text{for the product update rule} \tag{6.4}$$

Please note that the order of elements in S is important here. Even though Score Erosion finds optimal solutions (not only approximations) for both functions, a direct relation to the original MSDS problem with one of the four diversity functions is not apparent. Score Erosion does not concentrate on achieving high degrees of diversity but rather tries to discover a large amount of islands (depending on β).

Now that we have presented several heuristics to solve MSDS, the interesting question is which heuristic performs the best. This is investigated in the next two chapters.

Chapter 7

Experimental Evaluation on Artificial Data

This chapter contains a large amount of experimental evaluation of the algorithms presented in the previous chapters. All tests have been performed with artificially generated datasets that mimic activity islands, whose existence is assumed for at least molecular datasets. The datapoints were randomly distributed in the plane, and, in turn, several activity centers $c \in C$ were assigned and given a score value of 1. All other points are given scores that exponentially decrease with increasing distance to the chosen points. The width of a peak is controlled with the parameter ω:

$$\sigma(\boldsymbol{x}) = \sum_{c \in C} e^{-\frac{(x_1 - c_1)^2 + (x_2 - c_2)^2}{\omega}} \quad (7.1)$$

Figure 7.1 shows the used dataset with 10,000 data points and three activity spots, indicated by the green colored points.

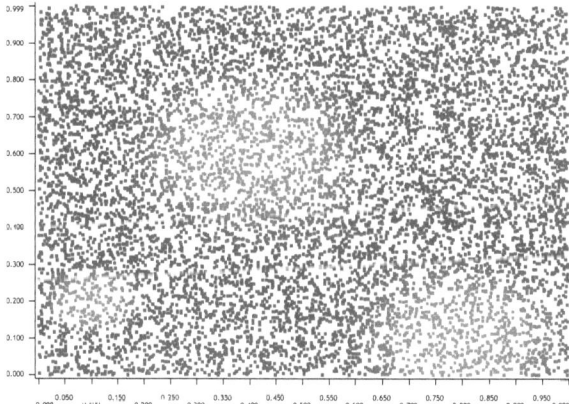

Figure 7.1: Artificial dataset with 10,000 points and three activity peaks.

All experiments were carried out in KNIME [8]. KNIME is a Java-based data analysis framework that permits the user to visually build workflows in which data is processed step-by-step by several nodes. Each algorithm was implemented as one (or several in the case of Score Erosion) nodes. KNIME was run with Sun's Java 1.6.0 on 64bit Linux computers having eight cores and 16 or 32 GB of memory.

The purpose of the experiments is to provide answers to the following questions:

- Which of the various genetic operators for subset selection presented in Chapter 5 is the preferred operator?

- Which of the presented heuristics (including the genetic algorithm) is the preferred one in terms of solution quality?

- What are the algorithms' runtimes in practice?

- How does the search space structure influence solution quality?

- How does the chosen diversity measure influence the distribution of the selected objects in MSDS?

In addition to these natural questions, another aspect is discussed that became apparent when we compared all heuristics with each other: the genetic algorithm approximated only a small part of the true Pareto front. Therefore we have also looked for a way to overcome this problem.

7.1 Influence of genetic representations and operators

As already mentioned, the genetic algorithm used was NSGA-II. The population size was set to 300 and mutation rate to 1% because these settings worked quite well. Each experiment was carried out 3 times. The number of individuals created during each run was 500,000 (which equals 1,667 generations). Even though the genetic algorithm was executed with eight parallel threads the experiments still took several days. The subset size p was set to 10% of the dataset size, i.e. 1,000 objects.

Figure 7.2 shows the Pareto fronts and the hypervolume evolution for the five genetic operators. The x-axis of the top diagram depicts the average score of all 1,000 objects in the selected set whereas the y-axis shows the subset's diversity, using p-dispersion-min-sum as the measure, divided by the number of selected objects (this normalization is used throughout all experiments in order to ensure compatible value ranges for both objectives). The bottom diagram shows the number of generated individuals on the x-axis and the hypervolume enclosed by the Pareto front approximations on the y-axis. For each operator two curves are shown, the best and the worst hypervolume evolution from all experiments.

Several observations can be made from these diagrams. First, uniform crossover with integer representation performs much better and the performance of all other operators is considerably worse. However, the maximal diversity values are similar for uniform, two-point, and SX

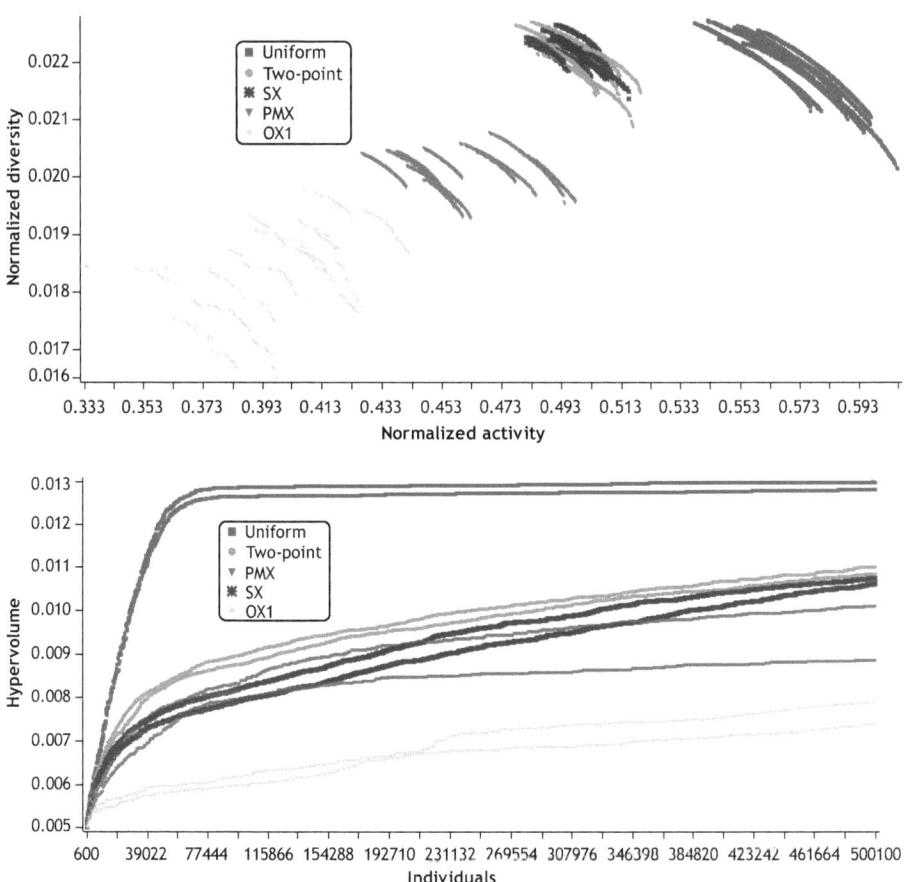

Figure 7.2: The Pareto front and the hypervolume evolution on the artificial dataset for up to 500,000 created individuals.

crossover. The choice of representation (binary (SX) or integer) for two-point crossover does not seem to have a great influence. The two permutation-based based operators do not perform nearly as well as the other operators. OX1 especially seems to shuffle the elements too much, preventing any proper convergence.

The hypervolume evolutions impressively demonstrate the superior convergence of the uniform crossover operator. Judging from the slopes of the curves it is expected that both two-point and SX crossover may at some point catch up with uniform crossover but for the dataset with 10,000 points this may take several days, which in most cases is unacceptable. Therefore the bigger the dataset the more advisable it is to use uniform crossover.

7.2 Deficiencies of the genetic algorithm

In the next section, in which different heuristic approaches for MSDS are compared with each other, we see that the Pareto fronts discovered by the genetic algorithms cover only a part of the true front, since the other algorithms find considerably larger fronts. Even after lots of further research and discussions with people from the MO community the cause for this effect is still unclear. It is common knowledge that algorithms such as NSGA-II acquire problems if the number of objectives increases, but with only two this is not an issue. Also potential pitfalls with genetic representations, which were already mentioned in Section 5.3.4, are unlikely to be a problem, because the two permutation based representations demonstrate exactly the same behavior. We found a way to at least partially fix this deficiency: adding the non-dominated solution, which consists of the top-p most highly scored objects to the initial population. The effect of this boost is depicted in Figure 7.3, showing the three Pareto fronts of the uniform crossover operator after 500,000 created individuals (as an example) with and without the boost. We can see that the genetic algorithms is now able to find much larger score-accentuated parts of the front. However, this comes at the expense of falling behind on the diversity-accentuated side of the front. As we explain later in the next chapter this behavior is not a general problem and for smaller datasets and/or more generations the loss of more diverse solutions is almost negligible.

Applying the boost has another remarkable effect: whereas before uniform crossover was clearly the best choice, the lead is now lost to the SX operator. Also all other operators are much closer, as can be seen in Figure 7.4. The two diagrams show the same set of experiments as before, the only difference being the applied boost.

To sum up the first set of experiments, two facts can be stated:

1. The novel uniform crossover operator for subset converges much faster than any other operator. This is especially useful in cases where the evaluation of one individual takes quite a long time. However, the lead is lost if the boost is applied.

2. The severe problems of the genetic algorithm to properly approximate the whole Pareto front can be partially overcome by adding corner solutions to the initial population. The

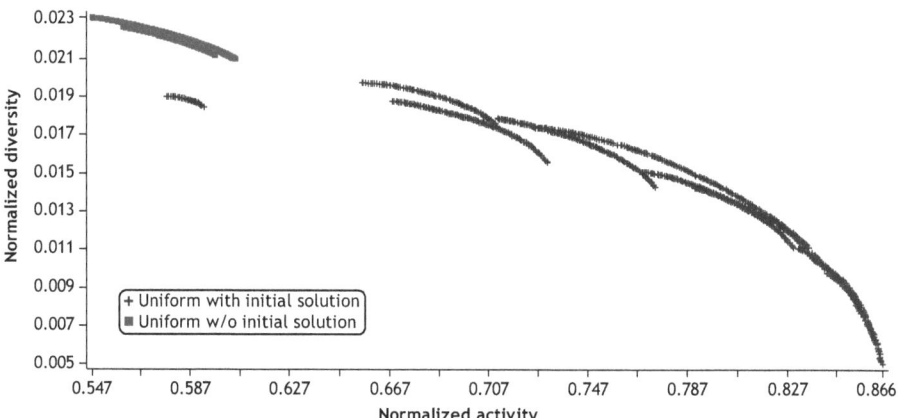

Figure 7.3: Adding the non-dominated solution with the most highly scored objects has a great impact in the discovered Pareto fronts.

reason for this deficiency is still unclear, because permutation based representations and operators, which do not lose objects like the other operators, behave even worse. Therefore the true reason is still unknown and may be a topic for further research.

7.3 Results with different heuristics

The second set of experiments compares the Pareto fronts created by all four heuristics — NSGA-II, Erkut's heuristic, Hochbaum&Shmoys' heuristic, and Score Erosion — with each other. This comprises an analysis of the approximated Pareto fronts as well as detailed runtime measurements.

The settings for the algorithms were as follows:

- The multi-objective genetic algorithm was run with using uniform crossover, 1% mutation rate, 300 individuals in one generation and 100,000 evolved individuals. We preferred this lower number for reasons of time and based it on the decreasing slope of the hypervolume curve in the previous experiments. The boost, involving adding the most highly scored subset, was applied. The GA was run four times, each time with a different diversity objective function.

- Erkut's heuristic was run after applying the edge label transformation described in Section 4.5. The parameter α is increased in steps of 0.01 from 0 up to 1. This algorithm is run twice, once for p-dispersion and once for p-dispersion-sum.

- For Hochbaum&Shmoys' p-center heuristic the same transformation and sampling as for Erkut's heuristic were used. The solutions shown are the best from eight random initializations.

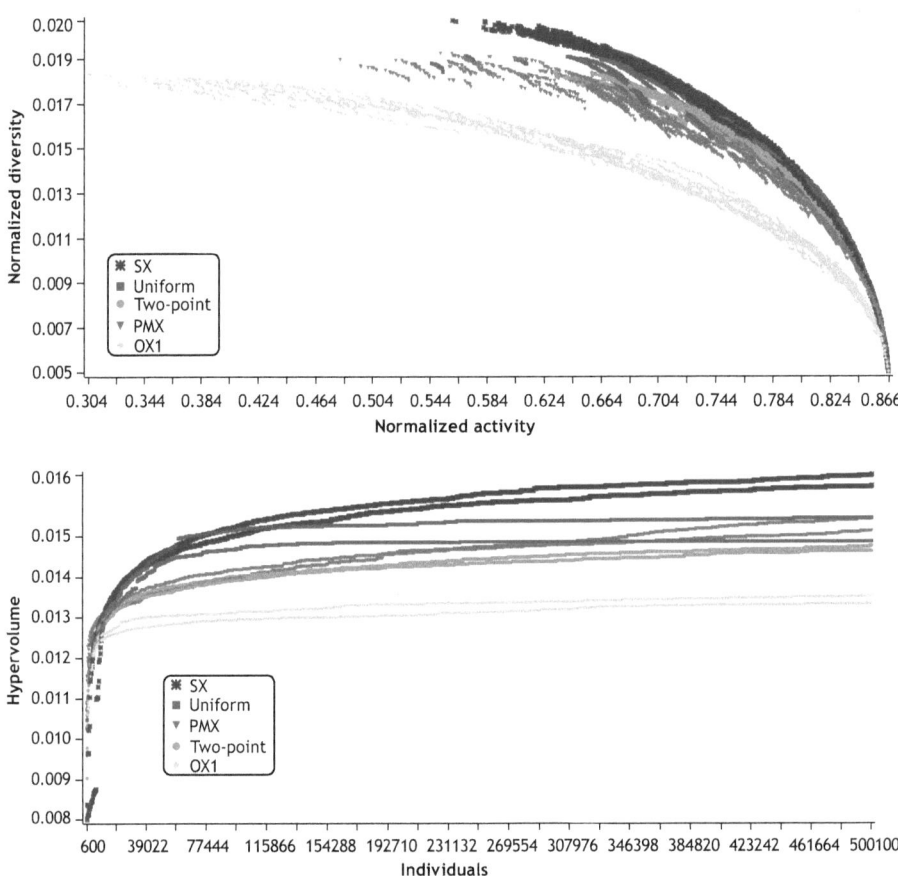

Figure 7.4: The Pareto front and the hypervolume evolution on the artificial dataset for up to 500,000 created individuals applying the boost.

- Score Erosion was run once with the product update rule and once with the difference update rule. In contrast to the other two heuristics and the experiments on molecular datasets in the following chapter, the range of β for Score Erosion was not chosen from 0 to 1. The artificial datasets contain many small distances and therefore the score values degrade very quickly even for small values of β. Therefore in the following experiments β was uniformly sampled from 0 to 0.08 (!) in steps of 0.0008.

The experiments presented in this section were performed on the same dataset as above. The subset size p was again set to 10% i.e. 1,000 objects.

7.3.1 Pareto front approximations

Figure 7.5 shows the solutions found for the six variants described above. Each diagram displays the results for a different diversity measure. Please note that the shown solutions are not necessarily proper approximations of the Pareto front since — except for the genetic algorithm — all solutions are displayed and not just the non-dominated ones.

Several observations can be derived from the diagrams.

- The distribution of solutions for both p-center and p-dispersion (first and second from from top) differs considerably in comparison to the solutions for p-dispersion-sum and p-dispersion-min-sum. One reason is that for p-center and p-dispersion several subsets can have the same diversity value but with different score values. This is caused by the min/max functions in their definitions.

- The genetic algorithm shows the already mentioned deficiencies in finding diverse solutions, *except* for p-center, for which it outperforms all other heuristics. This is a surprise since it is the other way round in all other three cases. The only plausible explanation is that the other heuristics behave badly in combination with this measure and the genetic algorithm's inferior solutions are not so apparent. However this is difficult to validate, as there is no other heuristic for comparison.

- For p-center the second best solutions are found by the p-center heuristic. At first glance it appears to be a little unusual that results are not as good as those from the genetic algorithm, despite the fact that there is a quality guarantee for the p-center heuristic. However, one has to keep in mind that due to the transformed edge labels (cf. Section 4.5) the optimized function is different to what should actually be optimized, and is plotted in the diagram. Interestingly, the p-dispersion variant of Erkut's algorithm also finds good solutions although the optimized function differs even more. The other three algorithms are unsuitable for p-center.

- The most diverse solutions for p-dispersion are created by Erkut's heuristic whereas the most highly scored solutions are discovered by both Score Erosion (using the product update rule) and the genetic algorithm. Score Erosion with the difference update rule

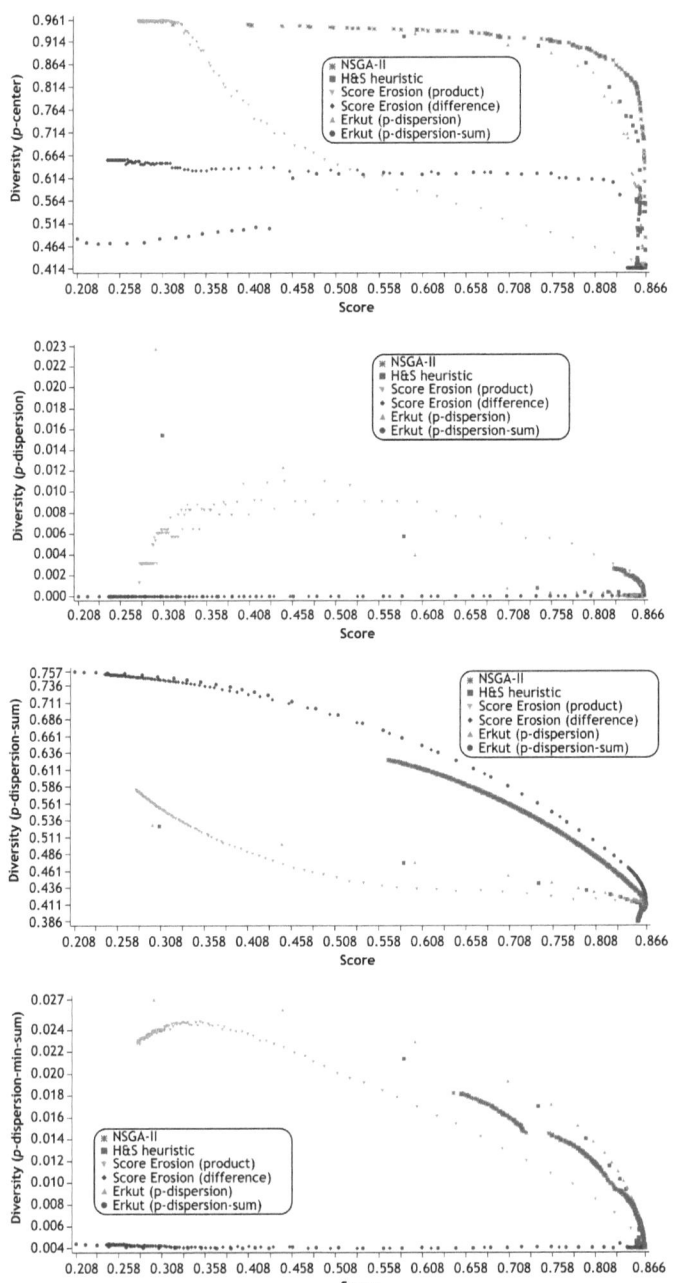

Figure 7.5: The four diagrams show the found solutions of different approaches with four different diversity measures (see labels on the y-axes) on the artificial dataset.

is unusable, as are Hochbaum&Shmoys' heuristic and Erkut's algorithm for p-dispersion-sum. This is no big surprise, since they are not designed to optimize the chosen diversity function.

- Solutions for p-dispersion-sum are almost equally well found by the genetic algorithm (again except for very diverse solutions), Erkut's heuristic and Score Erosion. Interestingly, this time the difference update rule performs much better than the product update rule.

- Last but not least the p-dispersion-min-sum objective is best optimized by the genetic algorithm for subsets with high scores and by Erkut's p-dispersion and Hochbaum&Shmoys' heuristic for diverse subsets. Score Erosion with the product update rule is slightly behind the genetic algorithm. The remaining approaches are much worse.

The performance of Score Erosion on this artificial dataset is a bit disappointing, especially since the construction of the dataset should favor Score Erosion's update rule. As we shall see in Section 7.4.1, this is very likely caused by the small number of activity peaks to which Score Erosion is quite sensitive. It is also apparent that values of β close to 0.08 do not increase diversity any more but instead often result in subsets that perform badly in both objectives. This is a clear indicator that the selection of objects becomes more or less random if many small distances are involved.

To sum up this set of experiments, there is no clear winner. Some heuristics perform better depending on the chosen diversity measure. Only the genetic algorithm can be recommended for all diversity measures while keeping in mind that except for p-center it misses parts of the Pareto front and never finds the best solutions.

7.3.2 Runtimes

In order to verify the runtime complexities of the heuristics, they were run on datasets of sizes 1,000 to 10,000. Each time three activity spots were created with the same parameters (location and width). This ensures that the search space structure remains almost the same for all experiments and only the number of objects varies. The runtimes were measured on an eight-core Intel system running at 1.83 GHz with 16GB main memory. The results are depicted in Figure 7.6.

As already mentioned, the reported runtimes for the genetic algorithm result from eight parallel threads, meaning that they are not directly comparable with the other heuristics. It is however obvious that the p-center measure is much more expensive to evaluate than the other measures (which are identical in complexity). Erkut's heuristic demonstrates the claimed quadratic increase (in fact $O(n^2 log n)$) in runtime well. Also the runtimes for Hochbaum&Shmoys' heuristic and for Score Erosion increase non-linearly in the number of objects but at a much lower rate. The fact that Score Erosion also shows a nonlinear increase lies in the fact that its complexity is $O(np)$ and since p was chosen to be $0.1n$ this also yields $O(n^2)$.

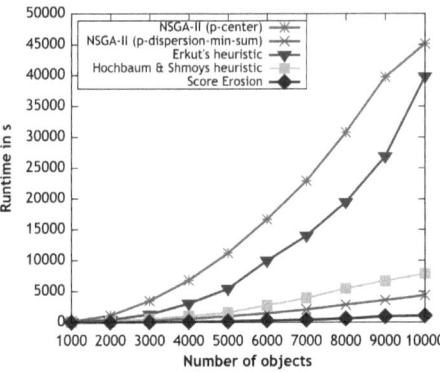

Figure 7.6: Runtimes of the four heuristics on increasing problem sizes.

The second part of the runtime analysis investigates the effect of p, the number of selected objects, on a constant-sized dataset of 2,000 objects. For Score Erosion linear increase in runtime is expected over the whole range of the experiment, whereas for the p-center heuristic the runtimes should show a slight increase (see Section 6.2 for the explanation). Erkut's heuristic should show a steep increase at the beginning and then get again faster at higher values of p since the local optimization (exchanging selected and unselected nodes) needs less time. Figure 7.7 demonstrates that our conjectures are right. Still, Score Erosion and the p-center

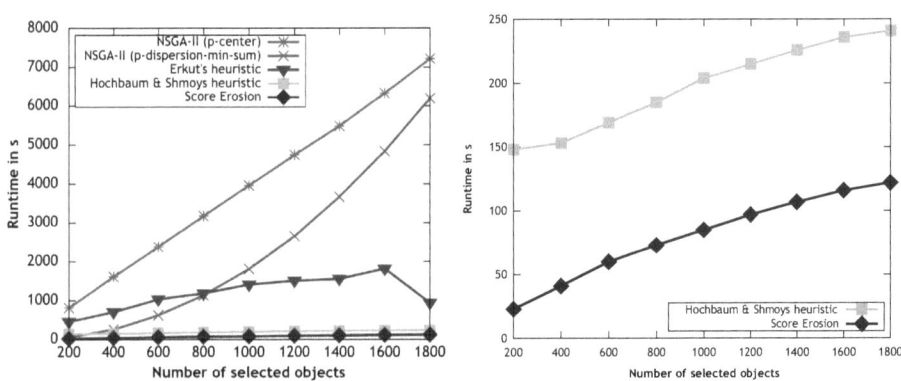

Figure 7.7: Runtime behavior of all heuristics with an increasing number of selected objects and a fixed dataset size. The right diagram shows a section from the bottom of the left diagram.

heuristic are much faster than Erkut's and in practice the selection of almost all objects from the complete set is rather uninteresting anyway.

7.4 Influence of the search space structure

Another advantage of using a 2D dataset is that the resulting subsets can easily be visualized and evaluated. One aspect that has not been covered yet is the structure of the search space. The motivation for MSDS was that both objectives are in conflict with each other meaning that similar objects have similar scores. There are two extreme cases: Either the objects show no neighborhood behavior, i.e. the scores are randomly distributed over all objects, or there is one single peak in the data where all highly scored objects are concentrated. Whereas the former poses a slightly easier problem, as selecting the most highly scored objects almost automatically results in a diverse subset, the latter seems to be the most complicated case because subsets that are more diverse than the top-p objects will always have a lower score.

Two important questions arise from this observation: First, does the search space structure (i.e. the number of peaks) influence the solutions' quality for the different algorithms, and second, how does the chosen diversity measure influence the created subsets.

7.4.1 Influence of peak count on solution quality

To answer the first question, twelve different artificial datasets were generated, containing up to twelve activity peaks. All algorithms were run on these datasets — with the same settings as in the previous experiments — and the approximated Pareto fronts were compared. Some of the results are shown in Figures 7.8 to 7.11. Each of the three diagrams in each figure shows the approximated Pareto fronts for one peak (top), six peaks (middle) and twelve peaks (bottom).

It is fairly obvious that the more peaks that are present, the easier it becomes to find solutions that contain both highly scored and diverse objects. The approximated fronts are much steeper on the right sides of the diagrams for the datasets with more peaks. Moreover, even if the maximal diverse subset has the same value regardless of the number of peaks the majority of solutions has much higher diversity values if more peaks are present. Comparing the individual algorithms, Score Erosion with the product update rule is very sensitive to the number of peaks. This becomes most obvious for the p-dispersion-min-sum measure where it easily outperforms all other heuristics with twelve peaks, except for Erkut's, however performance for only one peak is much worse.

7.4.2 Behavior of the diversity functions

In order to analyze the diversity functions' influence, another artificial dataset was generated that mimics a case where one huge activity peak is surrounded by some much smaller activity islands. The total number of points is 10,000 and the number of selected points 500 (we used a smaller number this time as the effects are much more apparent in this constellation). The remaining settings for all algorithms were the same as for the previous experiments on the artificial datasets.

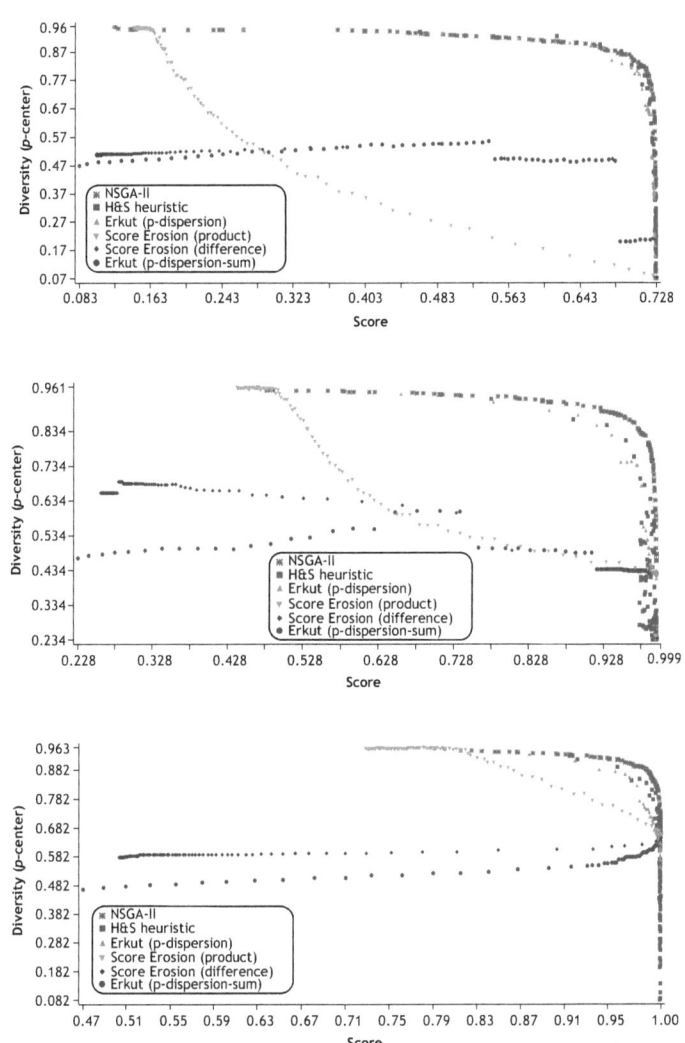

Figure 7.8: Approximated Pareto fronts for the *p*-center measure on datasets with one (top), six (middle), and twelve (bottom) peaks.

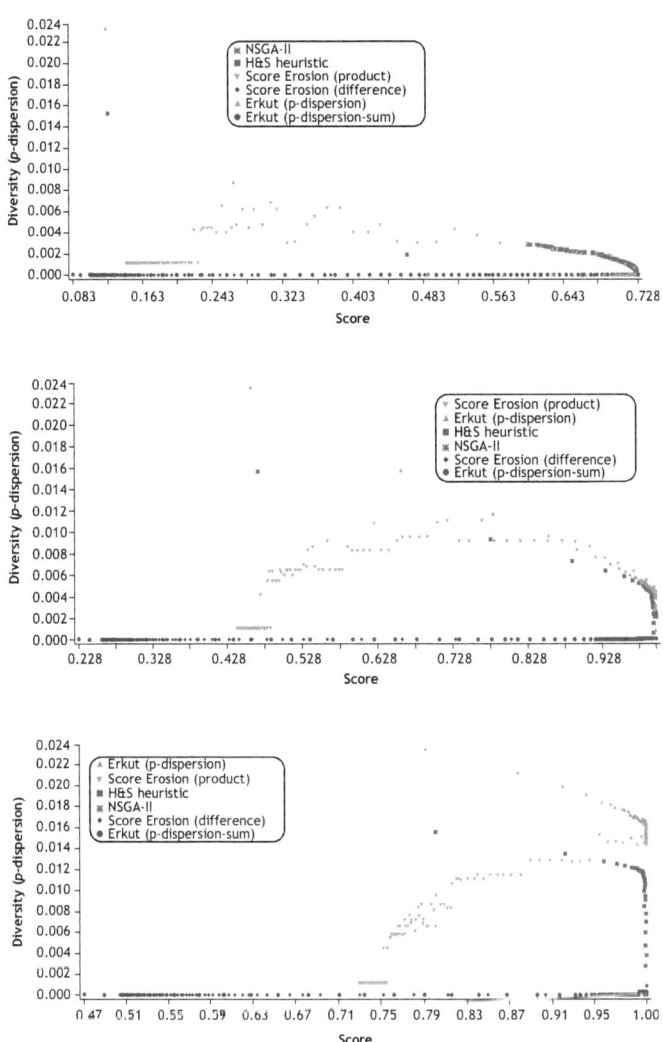

Figure 7.9: Approximated Pareto fronts for the p-dispersion measure on datasets with one (top), six (middle), and twelve (bottom) peaks.

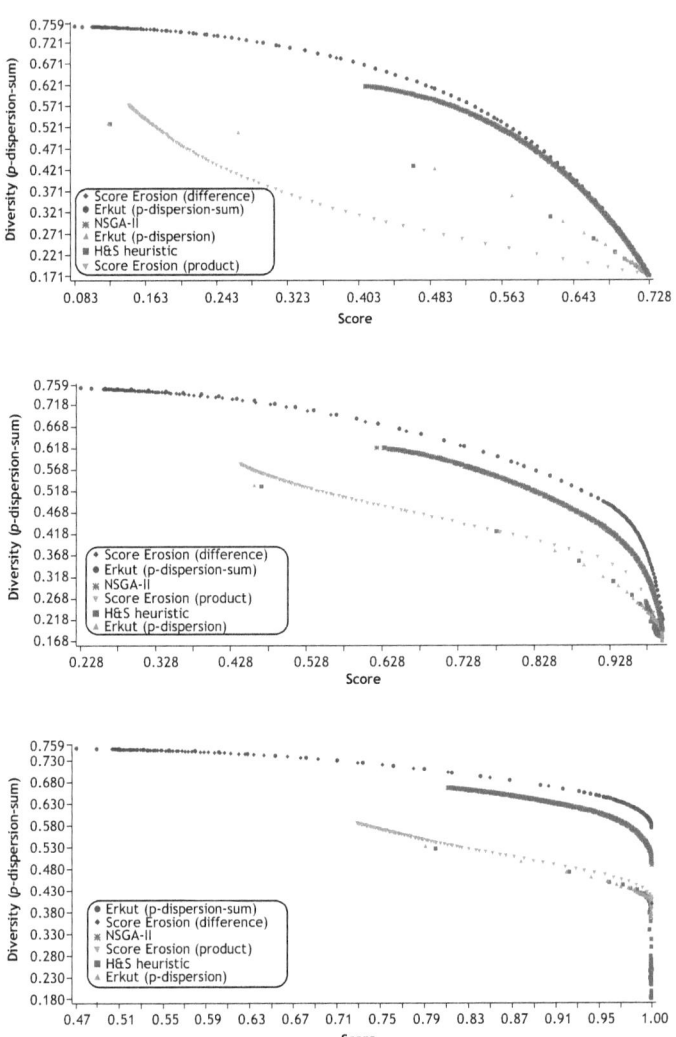

Figure 7.10: Approximated Pareto fronts for the p-dispersion-sum measure on datasets with one (top), six (middle), and twelve (bottom) peaks.

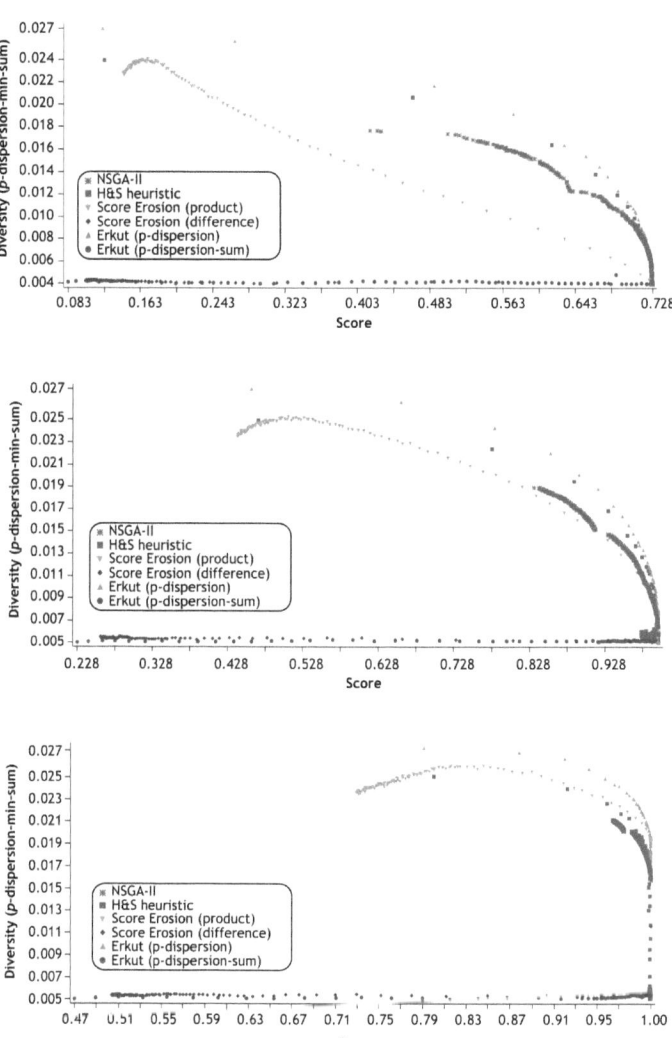

Figure 7.11: Approximated Pareto fronts for the p-dispersion-min-sum measure on datasets with one (top), six (middle), and twelve (bottom) peaks.

The naive approach of picking the top-p elements results in the distributions shown in Figure 7.12.

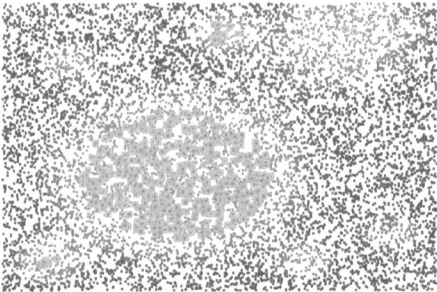

Figure 7.12: Sample distribution with the 500 most highly scored objects selected.

It is clearly visible that by far the most selected objects lie on the big activity peak whereas only three of the six smaller islands are sparsely covered. If their activities were only slightly less, they would not be covered at all. If MSDS worked as expected a reasonably well chosen subset would cover all islands with a significant amount of selected objects. Therefore the most diverse subsets in terms of the four diversity measures at a fixed score value were selected and the corresponding objects were marked in the 2D plot. Since the approximated Pareto fronts are often not very dense it was not possible to choose subsets with exactly the same score values. Instead, the most diverse subsets around a score value of 0.935 were selected. The

Table 7.1: Objective values of the selected subsets shown in Figure 7.13.

Diversity measure	Score value	Diversity value
p-dispersion	0.935	0.014
p-dispersion-sum	0.935	0.574
p-dispersion-min-sum	0.935	0.024
p-center	0.934	0.873

corresponding objective values are shown in Table 7.1 and the selected subsets are depicted in Figure 7.13.

All four diversity measures lead to the coverage of all six islands around the big peak. However, there are some obvious differences. p-dispersion shows the most appealing coverage since all islands contain several selected objects and the points within the islands are evenly distributed. p-dispersion-sum on the other hand again shows the undesired effect of clustering points. Coverage of the main peak is particularly degenerated. The subset optimized with p-dispersion-min-sum looks similar to p-dispersion, however the small peaks are not very well covered. It also tends to select the points more to the centers of the peaks. p-center also covers all peaks but with only very few points. Particularly the two latter diversity functions also lead to a few low scored objects being selected. Judging from this single experiment, p-dispersion is

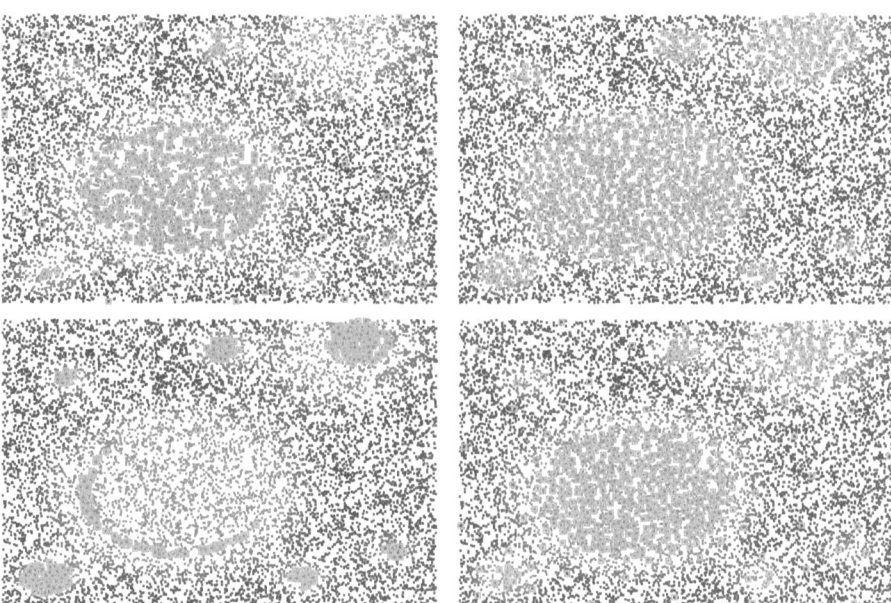

Figure 7.13: Sample distribution with optimized subsets according to the p-center (top-left), p-dispersion (top-right), p-dispersion-sum (bottom-left), and p-dispersion-min-sum (bottom-right) diversity measures.

the first choice, followed by p-dispersion-min-sum and p-center. p-dispersion-sum is clearly not an appropriate diversity measure in this case.

Even though the artificial datasets used in this chapter have provided many important answers to the questions posed at the beginning, the results cannot be directly transferred to any other dataset. Since the original motivation for MSDS was to select subsets of molecules, the next chapter tries to verify the results found so far on real-world molecular datasets.

Chapter 8

Experiments and Applications on Molecular Datasets

In this chapter MSDS is tested on molecules in two ways. First MSDS is used on three different molecular datasets to select subsets of molecules. Similar to the experiments in the previous chapter first the genetic operators are evaluated in Section 8.1.1 and then all four heuristics are compared against each other in Section 8.1.2. Another interesting question is if the usage of MSDS in fact supports the task of finding more potential lead structures for further improvement in lead optimization. This can be verified by looking at the number of covered molecule clusters in the found subsets, which is performed in Section 8.1.3. Finally Section 8.2 takes a look at how MSDS can be used for feature selection on discriminative molecular fragments.

8.1 MSDS on molecules

The first dataset, which is used throughout most experiments, is publicly available from BindingDB.org [43, 1] consisting of 1,376 molecules that have been tested for their activity against the CDK2 protein. The dataset contains the molecules' activities as IC_{50} values and their two-dimensional graph structure. Setting the subset size to 137 (10% of the database), results in a search space of about $1.8 * 10^{193}$ possible solutions.

The score values used in the experiments are derived from the IC_{50} values by normalizing them between 0 and 1. The score objective is easily computed by summing up all score values from the selected subset. The diversity objective is substantially harder to compute because first the pairwise distances between the molecules have to be computed. The MCSS-based measure described in Section 2.1 is used and all distances are computed in a preprocessing step. However, for larger datasets it may not be feasible to pre-compute distances any more because the distance matrix needs too much space. In some cases, especially for Score Erosion, only a small fraction of distances is actually needed during optimization, anyway. Thus it may be better to compute the distances on-the-fly.

The second, much bigger, dataset was taken from PubChem.[1] The bioassay with AID 884 contains 13,082 tested molecules. We filtered out all molecules that did not have a value for the activity at 0.457 μM, which we took as score values for the molecules (since the most molecules have been tested at this concentration). 12,156 compounds remained after this step. The third dataset is an in-house dataset from Nycomed consisting of 1,572 molecules with IC_{50} values.

The purpose of these experiments is twofold: First, to validate the results from the artificial dataset and/or make additional observations, and second to check whether MSDS is useful in practice when it comes to selecting new molecules for HTS.

8.1.1 Influence of genetic representations and operators

Since the CDK2 dataset is much smaller than the artificial dataset used before, we let the genetic algorithm create up to 10 million individuals and it was run 10 times. Figure 8.1 shows the Pareto fronts after $500,000$, $1,000,000$ and $10,000,000$ created individuals. The usage of a much larger number of individuals gives more insights into the behavior of the various genetic operators than the experiments on the artificial dataset. As before, uniform crossover with the integer representation performs much better in early stages of the algorithm, whereas the performance of all other operators is worse on average. After the creation of one million individuals, uniform crossover continues to take the lead, however differences become smaller. The picture finally reverses after 10 million individuals, where uniform crossover is outperformed by both two-point crossover variants (this was already suspected based on the slopes of the hypervolume curves). Not only are the fronts nearer to the optimum but their solutions are also spread more widely, especially on the diversity axis. The permutation-based operators continue to lag behind.

The improved convergence of uniform crossover in early stages can be seen even better when looking at the hypervolumes of the Pareto fronts. Figure 8.2 shows the hypervolume for the five different operators, for both the best and worst run. The top diagram shows a cutout of the first 100,000 individuals whereas the bottom figure shows the development until 10 million individuals.

As in the Pareto front plots, it is clear that uniform crossover converges much faster than all other operators. In the end it is finally outperformed, but only to a small amount, mainly due to solutions in the corners of the search space.

The genetic algorithm does not approximate the Pareto front well on this dataset, too, without the boost. Its effect is depicted in Figure 8.3, showing the 10 Pareto fronts of the uniform crossover operator after 1,000,000 created individuals (as an example) with and without the boost. It is clearly visible that the genetic algorithm is now able to find the score-accentuated part of the front completely. This allows for two important conclusions: first, this modification should be applied whenever possible and second, this supports the claim that metaheuristic are not always the best choice if details about the problem are known.

---

[1] http://pubchem.ncbi.nlm.nih.gov/

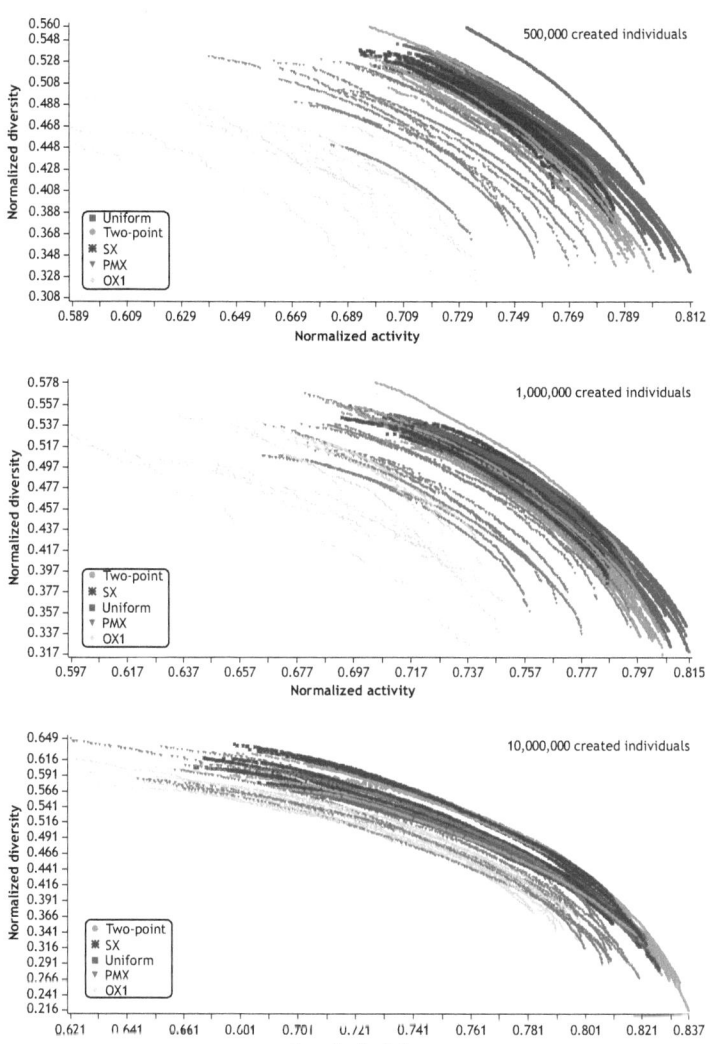

Figure 8.1: The three diagrams show the Pareto fronts created by the different genetic operators. The fronts are shown after 500,000, one million and ten million created individuals. Each diagram contains the fronts of 10 different runs.

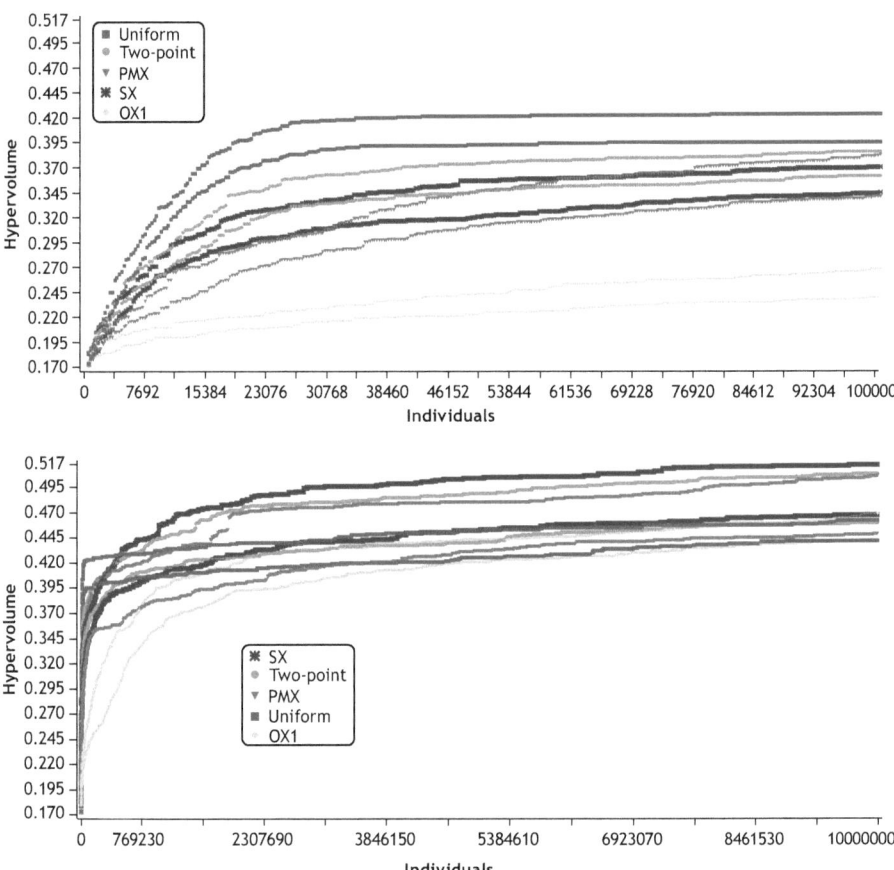

Figure 8.2: The hypervolume indicator for up to 100,000 created individuals (top) and for up to 10 million individuals (bottom). Uniform crossover converges much faster but is outperformed by two-point crossover in late generations

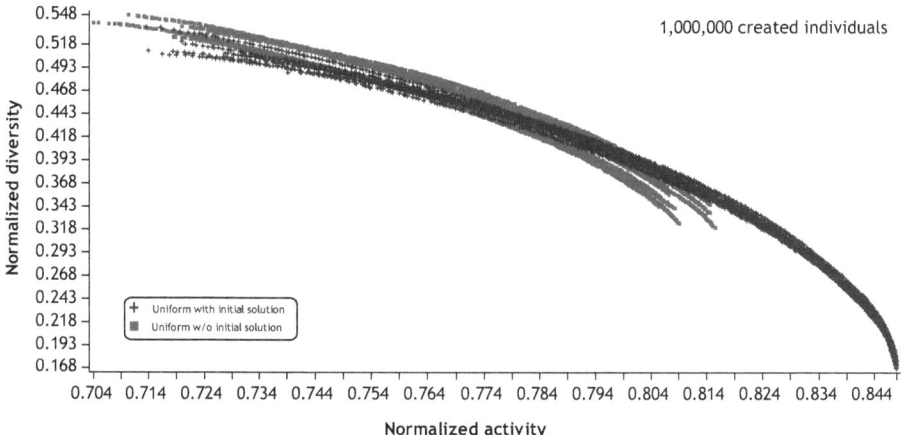

Figure 8.3: Adding the non-dominated solution with the most highly scored objects has a great impact on the discovered Pareto fronts.

The above experiments on the CDK2 dataset support the conclusion drawn so far from the experiments on the artificial dataset. In addition it has become apparent that in the long term both two-point crossover operators, the binary SX and the novel integer-array based operator, are able to evolve slightly better Pareto fronts than uniform crossover. If time is not an issue either of the two-point crossover operators is preferable.

8.1.2 Pareto front approximations

The second part of the experiments on the molecular datasets compares the results of all four heuristics. In the process, the Pareto fronts were approximated with the following algorithm settings:

- The multi-objective genetic algorithm using uniform crossover, 1% mutation rate, 300 individuals in one generation and 1,000,000 evolved individuals for CDK2 and 100,000 for both other datasets, respectively. The boost is applied, adding the most highly scored subset. The GA is run four times, each time with a different diversity objective function.

- Erkut's heuristic, applying the edge label transformation described in Section 4.5. The parameter α is increased in steps of 0.01 from 0 up to 1. This algorithm is run twice, once for p-dispersion and once for p-dispersion-sum.

- Hochbaum&Shmoys' p-center heuristic using the same transformation and sampling as for Erkut's heuristic. The shown solutions are the best from 8 random initializations.

- Score Erosion, once with the product update rule and once with the difference update rule. The β parameter is varied in the same way as for both other heuristics from 0 to 1.

Figure 8.4 shows the found solutions on the CDK2 dataset for the six variants described above. Each diagram shows the results for a different diversity measure.

The diagrams substantiate the conclusions that have already been drawn from the previous experiments on the artificial dataset. Two additional facts are noteworthy:

- Besides the lack of diverse subsets, the genetic algorithm always finds solutions that are non-dominated by any other solution. This is an indicator that the 500,000 individuals evolved on the artificial dataset were probably too few and that in later generations result would improve considerably.

- It is quite remarkable that the Pareto fronts approximated by the genetic algorithm, Score Erosion, *and* Erkut's heuristic are almost identical for p-dispersion-sum and p-dispersion-min-sum. Whereas this cannot be taken as proof, it is nevertheless a strong indicator that this may be the true Pareto front.

The results on the AID 884 dataset are comparable, as can be seen in Figure 8.5. Note that here, too, a number of differences are apparent. Once again, the genetic algorithm does not approximate the Pareto fronts as well. This can be due to the much larger number of possible subsets ($6.77 * 10^{1498}$) and the lower number of generations because the AID 884 dataset is about 10 times the size of the CDK2 dataset. Also, the results from the p-center measure appear to be a little unusual, as only about five classes of subsets with different p-center values are found. Also, the curves representing the approximated Pareto fronts have degenerated. Still, the genetic algorithm finds the best solutions in this case, too.

Behavior on the Nycomed dataset is also comparable, see Figure 8.6. The coverage by the genetic algorithm is again better than for the big AID 884 dataset. One fact about Score Erosion becomes apparent here: the β-parameter is quite dependent on the dataset. Whereas the range from 0 to 1 produces usable results for the first two datasets, this time the solutions get worse if β is above some threshold. This is seen clearly in the diagrams with the p-dispersion-min-sum measure where the Score Erosion curve sharply drops down for activity values below about 0.73.

Also on the molecular datasets, there is no clear winner. The genetic algorithm always finds high-quality solutions but is mostly restricted to more highly scored subsets. Also the size of the dataset and therefore the number of possible subsets has a great influence on the solution quality. The larger the search space the more difficult it becomes to find good solutions (with the same number of iterations). Erkut's heuristic (in the correct variant) finds solutions of comparable quality and is much better for diverse subsets. Except for p-center, where most heuristics perform poorly, Score Erosion with the product update rule is also a good choice, especially since it is much faster than the other approach. The p-center heuristic does not find high quality solutions at all.

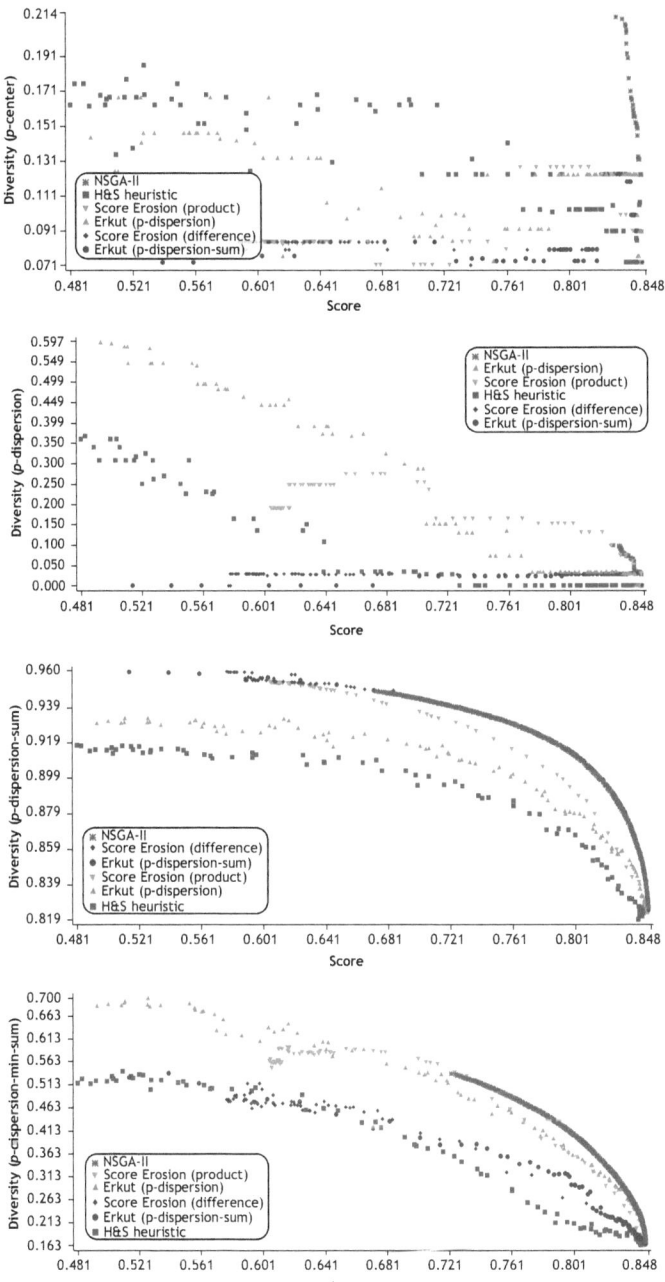

Figure 8.4: The four diagrams show the found solutions of different approaches with four different diversity measures (see labels on the y-axes) on the CDK2 dataset.

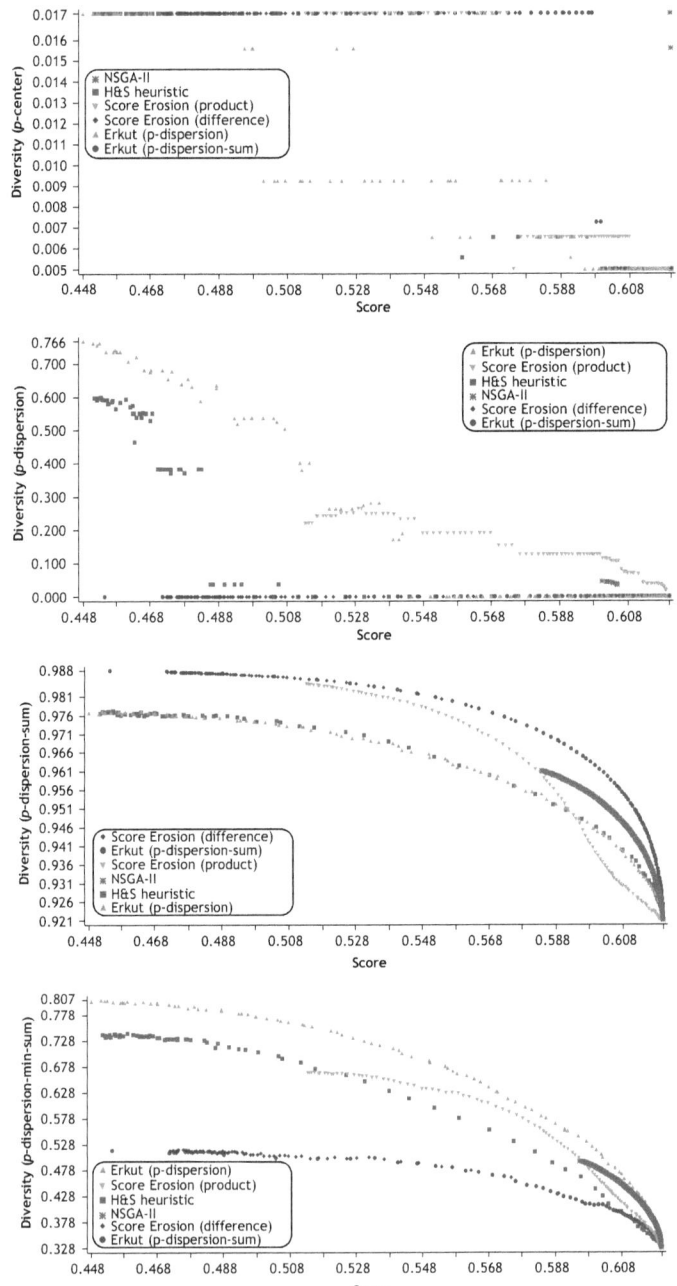

Figure 8.5: The four diagrams show the found solutions of different approaches with four different diversity measures (see labels on the y-axes) on the AID 884 dataset.

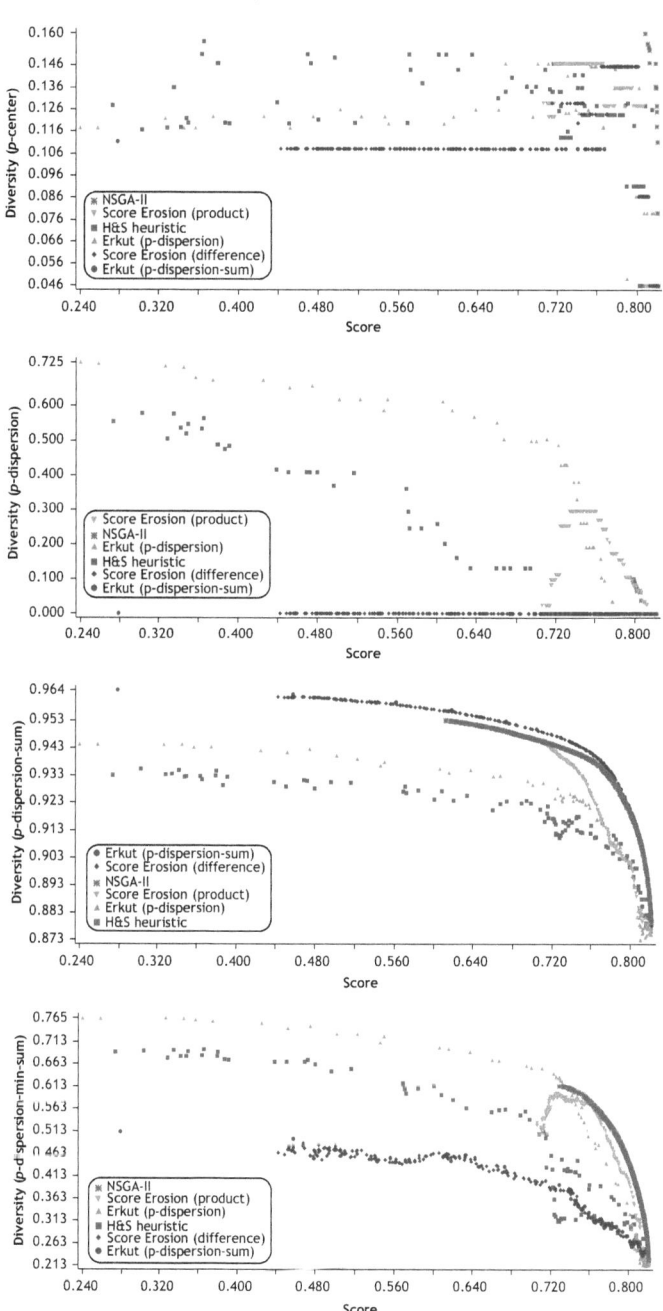

Figure 8.6: The four diagrams show the found solutions of different approaches measure with four different diversity measures (see labels on the y-axes) on the Nycomed dataset.

8.1.3 Practical results

The main motivation for MSDS was that an optimized subset is more diverse than pure "top-p" selection and is more active than a random or purely diverse subset. In HTS, chemists are usually interested in the number of molecule clusters that are covered. The more, the better since each cluster is a potential, independent starting point for further optimization. Therefore all molecules in the CDK2 dataset were assigned to clusters in the same way as for all real projects at Nycomed (aided by the *ClassPharmer*^{TM} program [62]), yielding 104 clusters. Then for each generated subset the number of clusters covered by its molecules was determined. Figure 8.7 shows the subsets' normalized activity plotted against the clusters count.

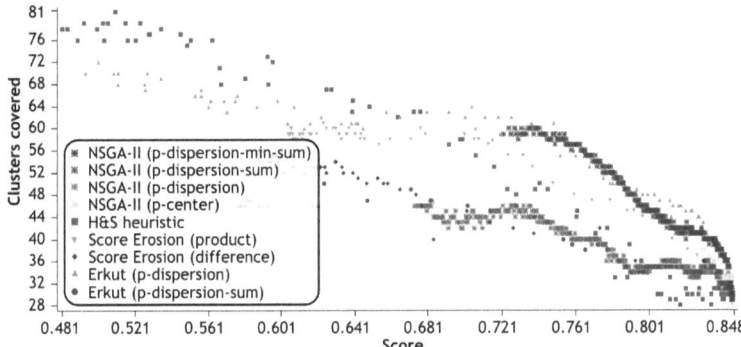

Figure 8.7: The number of covered clusters for the CDK2 dataset plotted against the activity value of all generated subsets.

These results are quite interesting, since the p-center heuristics discovers the most clusters by far, although with comparatively low scores. However, this does not imply that the p-center measure is best suited for molecules: First, the p-center values computed by the heuristics were rather low compared to e.g. the genetic algorithm. Second, the subsets generated by the GA with the p-center measure cover far less clusters although their p-center values are highest. It seems that the measure optimized by Hochbaum&Shmoys' heuristic (see Equation 4.27) is quite good for covering the defined clusters. However, one has to keep in mind that this behavior depends on the chosen clustering algorithm and other sensible clusterings may exist for which coverage is different. The remaining observations are similar to observations discussed above: Score Erosion with the product update rule works fairly well as does Erkut's p-dispersion heuristic.

However, the picture is different for the AID 884 dataset, as can be seen in Figure 8.8. As opposed to Hochbaum&Shmoys' heuristic, this time Score Erosion and Erkut's heuristics cover more clusters by far than any other approach. The fact that for Score Erosion the number of clusters falls down below an activity value of about 0.58 is due to an inappropriate choice of the β-parameter's range, which was already discussed above. The same holds for almost all other heuristics. Concerning the genetic algorithm, optimizing the p-dispersion-min-sum

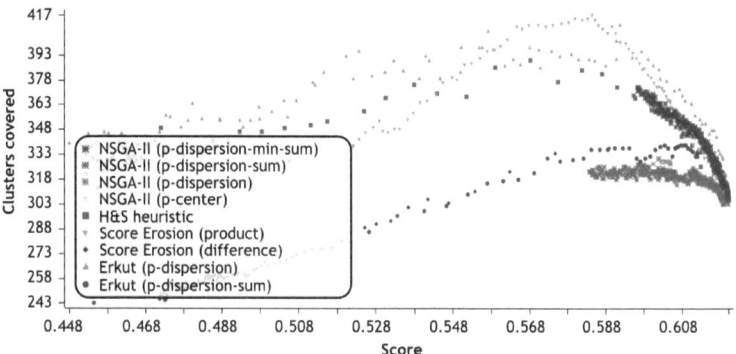

Figure 8.8: The number of covered clusters for the AID 884 dataset plotted against the activity value of all generated subsets.

measure gives the best results which is again an indication that this measure is the preferred one for molecular datasets.

The behavior is more or less the same on Nycomed's dataset, which is shown in Figure 8.9. It is apparent that in this case too, the p-dispersion-min-sum measure correlates the best with

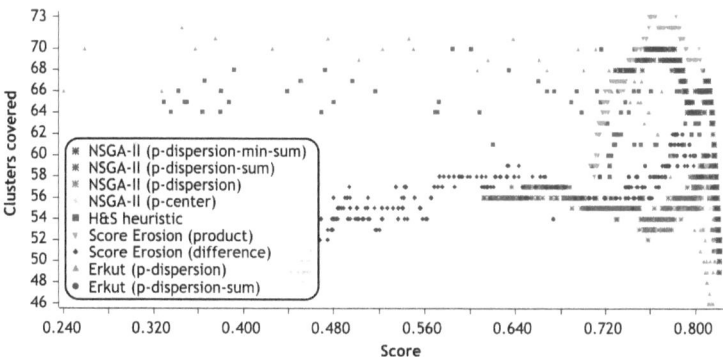

Figure 8.9: The number of covered clusters for the Nycomed dataset plotted against the activity value of all generated subsets.

the number of covered clusters as can be seen from the solutions found by the genetic algorithm with the corresponding diversity measure. Even better coverage is obtained by Score Erosion. The reason that this algorithm also produces many inferior solutions is once again attributed to the choice of the β parameter. It was steadily increased from 0 to 1 and higher values of β lead to worse solutions. In practice this is not a real problem since this effect is easily noticeable and can be compensated by an appropriate sampling of β. Since Score Erosion is by far the fastest heuristic one can easily experiment with different parameter settings.

8.2 MSDS for feature selection

We already mentioned in the introduction that MSDS can also be used to perform feature selection. This can be motivated by a use case from drug discovery. One possible way to predict the activities of molecules is to use a labeled dataset and search for discriminative fragments, i.e. fragments that occur often in active molecules and seldom in inactive ones (or the other way round). This is usually done with one of the subgraph mining algorithms already mentioned in Section 2.2. The resulting discriminative fragments are subsequently used to build a classifier. The simplest classifier checks to see if a discriminative fragment occurs in a molecule or not and labels it accordingly. One drawback of this approach is the fact that usually quite a lot of discriminative fragments are found, most of which are similar to each other. Therefore the number of fragments needs to be reduced. One way is to apply kernel methods to the set of frequent fragments [13, 23]. Another way is to apply MSDS to select a subset of fragments that is best suited for labeling unknown graphs. The selected fragments should on the one hand have a high lift (i.e. high ratio between active molecules and inactive molecules in which they occur) and be pairwise diverse on the other. A similar approach has been described in [69].

In order to verify that MSDS can indeed help in selecting a suitable subset of fragments, which are used as features in later classification tasks, we used PubChem's AID 1 dataset.[2] It consists of 40,877 unique compounds, 2,068 of which are classified as active and 100 unclassified molecules. MoSS (with the ring mining feature enabled) was subsequently used to search for fragments that occur in at least 1.5% of all active molecules and at most 5% of the inactive molecules. This may result in fragments that occur more often in inactive molecules than in actives ones but MSDS should be able to sort those out since their lift is very low (< 1). In total 2,906 frequent fragments were found.

Using all fragments for "predicting" active molecules on the same dataset results in 35,917 molecules classified as active, which is obviously a useless classification. Therefore MSDS is applied on the fragments to select a subset of 50 fragments. For this particular dataset the genetic algorithm and Erkut's heuristic found the best solutions therefore in the following figure only their solutions are shown.

In order to evaluate the quality of the simple classifiers that are built using any of the found subsets, the F-measure (or F-score) was used, mainly because it can handle imbalanced datasets better than other standard measures such as accuracy, precision, or recall. The F-measure (more precisely the F_1-measure) is defined as

$$F_1 = 2 \cdot \frac{precision \cdot recall}{precision + recall} \qquad (8.1)$$

---

[2] The positive effect of MSDS with such a simple classifier is not visible on all datasets. However, we choose not to apply a more sophisticated classifier since the results would then be more dependent on the chosen method and not on the MSDS itself.

with

$$precision = \frac{true\ positives}{true\ positives + false\ positives} \tag{8.2}$$

$$recall = \frac{true\ positives}{true\ positives + false\ negatives} \tag{8.3}$$

The active molecules constitute the positive class whereas the inactive molecules form the negative class. The prospect is that subsets that contain the top-50 molecules with the highest scores scores do not perform as well as subsets that are more balanced between highly scored and diverse subsets, because they cover only few active molecules. The same should hold for subsets that contain the most diverse fragments since they cannot distinguish between active and inactive molecules. And in fact, this behavior can be observed. Figure 8.10 shows the MSDS solutions for both the genetic algorithm (optimizing p-dispersion-min-sum) and Erkut's heuristic (for p-dispersion). The color indicates the F-measure of the subset when used in the

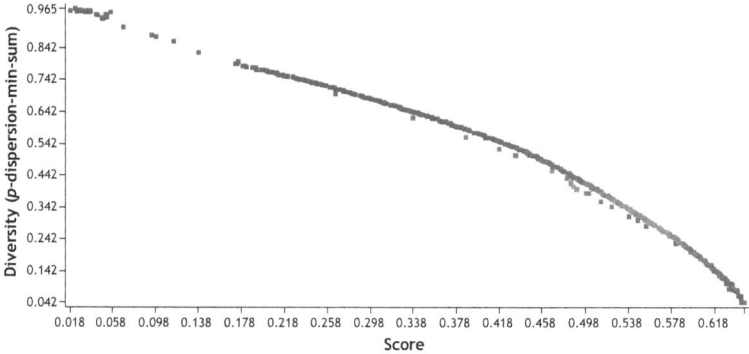

Figure 8.10: Pareto front for the fragments subsets, the color indicating the subset's F-scores.

simple classifier. Red is the lowest F-measure of 0.059 whereas green is the highest F-measure of 0.341. Of course, this value is not an excellent value, but bear in mind that the classificator is a very simple one. Furthermore, the point is not the absolute F-measures but rather the fact that there are significant differences between the subsets. It is clear that the most active subsets are the worst and the best subsets are found more to the middle of the Pareto front. The diverse subsets are also not good, but not as much as the highly scored subsets. The same can be seen if the F-measure is plotted on the y-axis instead of the diversity value, see Figure 8.11. There is a clear peak around score values of 0.53. The same behavior can be seen when p-dispersion-sum is optimized. p-dispersion and p-center do not show the effect as clearly.

This simple example has demonstrated that MSDS can also be quite useful in feature selection. On the one hand, subsets with highly scored features (very discriminative in the example above) yield a high precision but a low recall since they cannot find all positive objects. On the other hand, highly diverse subsets select objects more or less independently from their class since the features cannot distinguish well between positive and negative classes. Therefore fea-

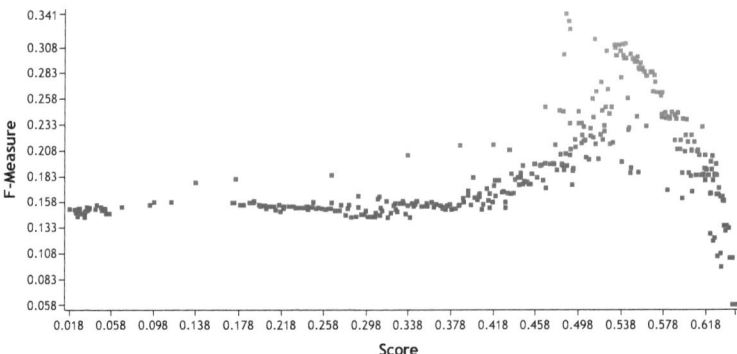

Figure 8.11: The subset's score plotted against their F-scores; the peak in the middle is clearly visible.

ture subsets that are balanced between score and diversity are much better suited for building a classifier.

Chapter 9
Conclusions

In this dissertation we have discussed the problem of Maximum-Score Diversity Selection. It has a broad applicability in chemoinformatics, economics, or in pattern mining and feature selection. We have shown that MSDS is a typical multi-objective optimization problem, consisting of two objectives: maximizing the score of the objects in the selected subsets and maximizing the subset's diversity. The first objective is easy to handle (once the scores are available) whereas the second objective is neither obvious to define nor to optimize. In general cases, where no special assumptions about the object's space are made but only a distance measure between a pair of objects is required, the first challenge is to define a diversity measure for a subset of points based on the pairwise distance relations. We have presented several existing definitions — p-dispersion, p-dispersion-sum and p-center — and proposed a simple yet intuitive measure, p-dispersion-min-sum. Further, we have proven that all four diversity measures lead to $\mathcal{NP}$-hard optimization problems, both in the single-objective and multi-objective case, in combination with the score objective.

Since these results rule out the usage of exact algorithms for practical dataset sizes of more than 100 objects, the only way to solve the problem of MSDS are heuristic approaches. One commonly used type of optimization algorithms, especially for multi-objective problems, are genetic algorithms. They do not operate on the problem directly, but merely need the individual objective functions for the problem with which they evaluate potential solutions. The solutions — subsets of objects in the case of MSDS — must be represented in a way that genetic operators can be applied to them to generate new solutions. Therefore we have developed several representations and genetic operators for subsets that are superior to existing approaches both in terms of computational efficiency and convergence in the optimization process.

However, genetic algorithms do not usually offer the best solution and as we have shown they suffer from two deficiencies: first their runtime is quite high — although this can be improved by parallelization, which is quite straight-forward for genetic algorithms — and second they are not capable of finding good approximations of the Pareto front but omit large parts. Therefore it is recommended to try out other heuristics that are specialized to the problem. Erkut's and Hochbaum&Shmoys' heuristics apply two algorithms that were originally invented to solve the single-objective problem of finding maximal diverse subsets for several diversity measures. We have shown a transformation to the input data so that these two approaches can also be used for MSDS. Even though the functions they are optimizing are not the same as if both objectives had been combined by the frequently applied weighting approach for multi-objective optimization problems, the results are quite satisfactory. Still both algorithms suffer from long runtimes and thus we have presented a novel heuristic called Score Erosion that runs much faster, is easier to implement and in most cases finds solutions of comparable quality.

In order to analyze the presented algorithms we carried out an extensive set of experiments. Several real-world molecular datasets were used to show the behavior in practice. Additional tests on synthetic data investigated the runtimes and the influence of the search space structure. The first part of the experiments compared the presented genetic representations. The novel integer-array-based representation together with uniform crossover showed by far the fastest convergence and was only slightly outperformed by the other representations in very late generations. Depending on population sizes and objective function complexity, this novel representation can therefore save a lot of computational time and resources.

The second batch of experiments compared all four heuristic approaches with each other. Probably the most important result was that the genetic algorithm was not able to approximate the Pareto front in its full breadth. Even with the boost of adding the most highly scored subset to the initial population it missed large parts of the more diverse region of the front. The second most important finding was that algorithm performance depends heavily on the chosen diversity measure. For p-center surprisingly the genetic algorithm performed best. Erkut's heuristic discovered one of the best solutions for the other three diversity measures. Score Erosion was best for p-dispersion, or close, for the other three measures. This behavior was consistent over all used molecular datasets. The picture slightly changed on the synthetic datasets. All heuristics showed the expected improved performance the more activity peaks were present in the dataset. The most sensitive reaction was observed for Score Erosion.

The runtime experiments confirmed the claims that Score Erosion is the fastest of all heuristics, followed by Hochbaum&Shmoys' heuristic. Erkut's heuristic is considerably slower as is the genetic algorithm, especially for the p-center measure, although this was already run eight-fold in parallel.

The final question was which diversity function is best suited for MSDS. Judging from the experiments on the molecular datasets, where the number of covered clusters was used as quality criterion, the p-dispersion-min-sum measure is the best choice as it showed the best correlation between diversity and the number of covered clusters. On the synthetic datasets visual inspection also showed that both good solutions for p-dispersion-min-sum and p-dispersion were best able to sufficiently cover all activity peaks.

We further discussed the application of MSDS in the drug discovery process in more detail. Especially the determination of sensible distances between molecules is crucial. As we have shown in the experiments, the chosen MCSS-based measure works quite well in practice. The computation of the MCSS, which is another $\mathcal{NP}$-hard problem, can be done efficiently by using a frequent subgraph mining algorithm. Several extensions that were originally developed for mining closed fragments are also useful for quickly discovering the MCSS between two molecules.

Finally, we want to point out the three most important aspects of this thesis:

- Defining a suitable measure for diversity is not straight-forward and most definitions lead to $\mathcal{NP}$-hard optimization problems. Among the presented measures p-dispersion-min-sum is the preferred measure.

- Genetic algorithms are a universal tool for solving all kinds of optimization problems. However, one should not solely rely on them as they can easily miss many good solutions, even when some assistance is provided.

- Score Erosion is a very fast heuristic for MSDS. It may not create the best solutions in all cases but is often comparable to other heuristics or even superior. For very large datasets and if time is an issue it is clearly the method of choice.

Appendix A

Complexity Theoretic Preliminaries

Although most readers should have heard about the theory of $\mathcal{NP}$-completeness, quite often the knowledge is only vague. Since it plays an essential role for this thesis, we shall repeat the most important facts, which are taken from [27], probably the best starting point for getting in touch with $\mathcal{NP}$.

The concept of complexity classes, of which $\mathcal{NP}$ is one, is based on Turing machines and decision problems. In contrast to optimization problems, where a specific optimal solutions is sought, decision problems have only answers, "yes" or "no". However, each optimization problem can be simulated by a sequence of decision problems by asking questions such as "is there a solution that has cost at most x". If a deterministic Turing machine (DTM) exists, which is able to solve a decision problem instance within a number of steps polynomially bounded by the length of the problem description, it can be said that this problem belongs to the $\mathcal{P}$ class. Informally, it consists of all problems that can be solved in polynomial time by a DTM (and therefore each standard computer). Deterministic means that the Turing machine will always perform the same steps and return the same result for the same input. Problems in $\mathcal{P}$ are said to be easy problems because there are efficient algorithms for solving them. Please note that use of the term "efficient" is rather loose here, as an algorithm that needs 'n^{10} steps, for example, is no longer particularly efficient.

The class $\mathcal{NP}$ consists of decision problems that can be solved by a *non-deterministic* Turing machine (NDTM) with a polynomially bounded number of steps. The big difference is that an NDTM can guess a solution and then check if it is a "yes" or "no" answer to the original question. Both guessing and checking are still polynomially bounded by the input size. This implies that the checking procedure, i.e. deciding if a solution yields a positive answer or not is in $\mathcal{P}$. Clearly, any problem solvable by DTM can also be solved by NDTM, i.e. $\mathcal{P} \subseteq \mathcal{NP}$. Roughly speaking, $\mathcal{NP}$ consists of all problems for which it is possible to *verify* positive solutions with a polynomial number of steps (but not to actually find them). The formal definition also includes that fact that only "yes"-instances can be checked in polynomial time, but "no"-instances need not. The big flaw of this model is, however, that in reality the non-deterministic guessing unit does not exist. It can only be simulated by a deterministic algorithm that needs an exponential number of steps.

The term $\mathcal{NP}$-complete refers to problems in $\mathcal{NP}$ that are the most hard to solve, i.e. if a problem is $\mathcal{NP}$-complete there is no problem in $\mathcal{NP}$ that is harder. This implies that not all problems in $\mathcal{NP}$ are $\mathcal{NP}$-complete and in fact all problems in $\mathcal{P}$ are not $\mathcal{NP}$-complete, as are various problems that are neither in $\mathcal{P}$, nor $\mathcal{NP}$-complete, such as the graph isomorphism problem. Along with $\mathcal{NP}$-completeness comes the term of *reducibility*, because the whole theory of it is based on reductions. A reduction is a transformation from a problem P to another problem P'. An algorithm or Turing machine that solves P' can subsequently be used to solve P, by applying the transformation beforehand. Usually it is assumed that these transformations run in polynomial time. If this is the case (and only if!), proving that a problem P' is $\mathcal{NP}$-complete essentially involves finding a suitable transformation from a known $\mathcal{NP}$-complete problem P to P'. If we were able to find an algorithm for P' that would run in polynomial time, we would be able to solve P in polynomial time as well, by applying the (polynomial-time) transformation beforehand. This, however, would be a contradiction to the proven $\mathcal{NP}$-completeness of P.

A popular reduction technique is *restriction*. The problem under consideration P' is restricted, by e.g. allowing only certain values for its parameters so that it becomes identical to a known $\mathcal{NP}$-complete problem P. One example is the *directed* Hamiltonian circuit problem. If the the edge set is restricted so that each directed edge (u, v) only occurs together with its counter-edge (v, u) the resulting problem is equal to the $\mathcal{NP}$-complete (undirected) Hamiltonian circuit problem. Thus the directed problem has to be $\mathcal{NP}$-complete, too.

Note that the fact that a problem is $\mathcal{NP}$-complete does not imply that *all* instances are hard to solve. It merely means that there is no deterministic Turing machine that can solve *all* possible instances in polynomial time.

The last term that frequently appears in discussion around $\mathcal{NP}$ is $\mathcal{NP}$-hard. There is again a considerable amount of theory around it, but it can be condensed to several facts:

- $\mathcal{NP}$-hard problems are "at least as hard" as $\mathcal{NP}$-complete problem, but they need *not* be in $\mathcal{NP}$

- The definition is not restricted to decision problems any more but merely to the more general optimization problems

- All $\mathcal{NP}$-complete problems are by definition also $\mathcal{NP}$-hard problems.

To conclude this (very) short introduction to the theory of $\mathcal{NP}$-completeness, Figure A.1 illustrates the relation between the sets of $\mathcal{P}$, $\mathcal{NP}$, $\mathcal{NP}$-complete, and $\mathcal{NP}$-hard. Note that this figure is only true under the assumption that $\mathcal{P} \neq \mathcal{NP}$. Otherwise $\mathcal{P}$, $\mathcal{NP}$ and $\mathcal{NP}$-complete would be equal.

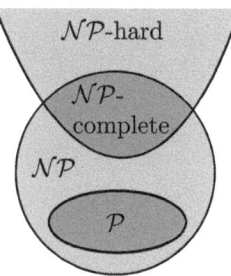

Figure A.1: Relations between the four most important complexity classes.

Bibliography

[1] BindingDB.org. http://www.bindingdb.org/. [Online; accessed 2007-05-24].

[2] S. F. B. Abolmaalia, J. K. Wegner, and A. Zell. The compressed feature matrix – a fast method for feature based substructure search. *Journal of Molecular Modeling*, 9(4):471–490, August 2003. doi: 10.1007/s00894-003-0126-0.

[3] F. N. Abu-Khzam, N. F. Samatova, M. A. Rizk, and M. A. Langston. The Maximum Common Subgraph Problem: Faster Solutions via Vertex Cover. In *Proceedings of ACS/IEEE International Conference on Computer Systems and Applications*, pages 367–373, Los Alamitos, CA, USA, 2007. IEEE Computer Society. doi: 10.1109/AICCSA.2007.370907.

[4] D. K. Agrafiotis. Stochastic Algorithms for Maximizing Molecular Diversity. *Journal of Chemical Information and Computer Sciences*, 37(5):841–851, September 1997. doi: 10.1021/ci9700337.

[5] J. Alvarez and B. Shoichet, editors. *Virtual Screening in Drug Discovery*. CRC Press, Boca Raton, FL, USA, 2005.

[6] R. Aringhieri, R. Cordone, and Y. Melzani. Tabu Search versus GRASP for the maximum diversity problem. *4OR: A Quarterly Journal of Operations Research*, 6(1):45–60, March 2008. doi: 10.1007/s10288-007-0033-9.

[7] A. Bender. *Studies on Molecular Similarity*. PhD thesis, University of Cambridge, 2005.

[8] M. R. Berthold, N. Cebron, F. Dill, T. R. Gabriel, T. Kötter, T. Meinl, P. Ohl, K. Thiel, and B. Wiswedel. KNIME - The Konstanz Information Miner. *SIGKDD Explorations*, 11(1), 2009.

[9] N. Beume, C. M. Fonseca, M. López-Ibáñez, L. Paquete, , and J. Vahrenhold. On the Complexity of Computing the Hypervolume Indicator. *IEEE Transactions on Evolutionary Computation*, 13(5):1075–1082, Oct. 2009. doi: 10.1109/TEVC.2009.2015575.

[10] C. Borgelt. On Canonical Forms for Frequent Graph Mining. In *Workshop on Mining Graphs, Trees, and Sequences at PKKD 2005*, pages 1–12, 2005.

[11] C. Borgelt and M. R. Berthold. Mining Molecular Fragments: Finding Relevant Substructures of Molecules. In *Proceedings of the IEEE Intl. Conf. on Data Mining ICDM*, pages 51–58, Piscataway, NJ, USA, 2002. IEEE Press.

[12] C. Borgelt and T. Meinl. Full Perfect Extension Pruning for Frequent Subgraph Mining. In D. A. Zigheda, S. Tsumoto, Z. W. Ras, and H. Hacid, editors, *Mining Complex Data*, volume

165 of *Studies in Computational Intelligence*, pages 189–205. Springer, Berlin, Germany, 2009. doi: 10.1007/978-3-540-88067-7_11.

[13] K. M. Borgwardt. *Graph Kernels*. PhD thesis, LMU München, 2007.

[14] C. Bron and J. Kerbosch. Algorithm 457: finding all cliques of an undirected graph. *Communications of the ACM*, 16(9):575–577, 1973. doi: 10.1145/362342.362367.

[15] J.-S. Chen and J.-L. Hou. A Combination Genetic Algorithm with Applications on Portfolio Optimization. In *Advances in Applied Artificial Intelligence*, volume 4031 of *Lecture Notes in Computer Science*, pages 197–206. Springer, Berlin, Germany, 2006. doi: 10.1007/11779568.

[16] C. A. C. Coello, G. B. Lamont, and D. A. V. Veldhuizen. *Evolutionary Algorithms for Solving Multi-Objective Problems*. Genetic and Evolutionary Computation. Springer Science+Business Media, 2 edition, 2007.

[17] B. Cuissart and J.-J. Hébrard. A Direct Algorithm to Find a Largest Common Connected Induced Subgraph of Two Graphs. In *Graph-Based Representations in Pattern Recognition*, volume 3434 of *Lecture Notes in Computer Science*, pages 162–171. Springer Berlin / Heidelberg, 2005. doi: 10.1007/b107037.

[18] C. Darwin. *On the origin of species*. John Murray, London, 1859.

[19] I. Das and J. E. Dennis. A closer look at drawbacks of minimizing weighted sums of objectives for Pareto set generation in multicriteria optimization problems. *Structural and Multidisciplinary Optimization*, 14(1):63–69, August 1997. doi: 10.1007/BF01197559.

[20] L. Davis. Applying Adaptive Algorithms to Epistatic Domains. In *Proceedings of the International Joint Conference on Artificial Intelligence*, pages 162–164, 1985.

[21] K. Deb, A. Pratap, S. Agarwal, and T. Meyarivan. A Fast and Elitist Multiobjective Genetic Algorithm: NSGA-II. *IEEE Transactions on Evolutionary Computation*, 6:182–197, 2002. doi: 10.1109/4235.996017.

[22] F. Dellacroce, A. Grosso, and M. Locatelli. A heuristic approach for the max–min diversity problem based on max-clique. *Computers & Operations Research*, 36(8):2429–2433, August 2009. doi: 10.1016/j.cor.2008.09.007.

[23] M. Deshpande, M. Kuramochi, N. Wale, and G. Karypis. Frequent Substructure-Based Approaches for Classifying Chemical Compounds. *IEEE Transactions on Knowledge Discovery and Data Engineering*, 17(8):1036–1050, 2005. doi: 10.1109/TKDE.2005.127.

[24] E. Erkut. The discrete p-dispersion problem. *European Journal of Operational Research*, 46(1):48–60, May 1990. doi: 10.1016/0377-2217(90)90297-O.

[25] M. Ester, H. peter Kriegel, and X. Xu. A density-based algorithm for discovering clusters in large spatial databases with noise. In E. Simoudis, J. Han, and U. Fayyad, editors, *Proc. of 2nd International Conference on Knowledge Discovery and Data Mining*, pages 226–231. AAAI Press, 1996.

[26] D. Garcia, N. Corral, and J. Canon. Combining Inter- and Intrapopulation Information with the Weitzman Approach to Diversity Conservation. *J Hered*, 96(6):704–712, November 2005. doi: 10.1093/jhered/esi103.

[27] M. R. Garey and D. S. Johnson. *Computers and Intractability: A Guide to the Theory of NP-Completeness*. W. H. Freeman and Company, 1979.

[28] H. Giersiefen, R. Hilgenfeld, and A. Hillisch. *Modern Methods of Drug Discovery*, chapter Modern methods of drug discovery: An introduction, pages 1–18. Birkhäuser Verlag, Basel, Switzerland, 2003.

[29] F. Glover and D. C. Sommer. Pitfalls of Rounding in Discrete Manegement Decision Problems. *Decision Sciences*, 6(2):211–220, 1975. doi: 10.1111/j.1540-5915.1975.tb01014.x.

[30] D. E. Goldberg and R. Lingle. Alleles, loci and the TSP. In J. J. Grefenstette, editor, *Proceedings of the First International Conference on Genetic Algorithms and Their Applications*, pages 154–159, Hillsdale, New Jersey, USA, 1985. Lawrence Erlbaum.

[31] S. L. Hakimi. Optimum Distribution of Switching Centers in a Communication Network and Some Related Graph Theoretic Problems. *OPERATIONS RESEARCH*, 13(3):462–475, May 1965. doi: 10.1287/opre.13.3.462.

[32] J. Han, H. Cheng, D. Xin, and X. Yan. Frequent pattern mining: current status and future directions. *Data Mining and Knowledge Discovery*, 15(1):55–86, August 2007. doi: 10.1007/s10618-006-0059-1.

[33] H. Hofer, C. Borgelt, and M. R. Berthold. Large Scale Mining of Molecular Fragments with Wildcards. *Intelligent Data Analysis*, 8(5):495–504, 2004.

[34] J. Horn, N. Nafpliotis, and D. E. Goldberg. A Niched Pareto Genetic Algorithm for Multiobjective Optimization. In *Proceedings of the First IEEE Conference on Evolutionary Computation, IEEE World Congress on Computational Intelligence*, pages 82–87, 1994. doi: 10.1109/ICEC.1994.350037.

[35] J. Huan, W. Wang, and J. Prins. Efficient Mining of Frequent Subgraphs in the Presence of Isomorphism. In *Proceedings of the 3rd IEEE Intl. Conf. on Data Mining ICDM*, pages 549–552, Piscataway, NJ, USA, 2003. IEEE Press. doi: 10.1109/ICDM.2003.1250974.

[36] O. Kariv and S. L. Hakimi. An Algorithmic Approach to Network Location Problems. I: The p-centers. *SIAM Journal on Applied Mathematics*, 37(3):513–538, December 1979. doi: 10.1137/0137040.

[37] V. Klee and G. J. Minty. How good is the simplex algorithm? In O. Shisha, editor, *Inequalities*, volume III, pages 159–175. Academic Press, New York, 1972.

[38] J. Knowles and D. Corne. On Metrics for Comparing Non-Dominated Sets. In *Proceedings of the 2002 Congress on Evolutionary Computation Conference*, pages 711–716, Los Alamitos, CA, USA, 2002. IEEE Computer Society. doi: 10.1109/CEC.2002.1007013.

[39] I. Koch. Enumerating all connected maximal common subgraphs in two graphs. *Theorectical Computer Science*, 250(1-2):1–30, 2001. doi: 10.1016/S0304-3975(00)00286-3.

[40] E. B. Krissinel and K. Henrick. Common subgraph isomorphism detection by backtracking search. *Software – Practice & Experience*, 34(6):591–607, 2004. doi: 10.1002/spe.588.

[41] P. Larrañaga, C. M. H. Kuijpers, R. Murga, I. Inza, and S. Dizdarevic. Genetic Algorithms for the Travelling Salesman Problem: A Review of Representations and Operators. *Artificial Intelligence Review*, 13(2):129–170, April 1999. doi: 10.1023/A:1006529012972.

[42] M. Laumanns, L. Thiele, K. Deb, and E. Zitzler. Combining Convergence and Diversity in Evolutionary Multiobjective Optimization. *Evolutionary Computation*, 10(3):263–282, September 2002. doi: 10.1162/106365602760234108.

[43] T. Liu, Y. L. X. Wen, R. N. Jorissen, and M. K. Gilson. BindingDB: a web-accessible database of experimentally determined proteinligand binding affinities. *Nucleic Acids Research*, 35:D198–D201(1), January 2007. doi: 10.1093/nar/gkl999.

[44] G. M. Maggiora and V. Shanmugasundaram. Molecular Similarity Measures. In J. Bajorath, editor, *Chemoinformatics - Concepts, Methods, and Tools for Drug Discovery*, volume 275 of *Methods in Molecular Biology*, pages 1–50. Humana Press, 2004. doi: 10.1385/1-59259-802-1:001.

[45] S. W. Mahfoud. *Niching Methods for Genetic Algorithms*. PhD thesis, University of Illinois at Urbana-Champaign, May 1995.

[46] K. V. Mardia. Some properties of classical multi-dimensional scaling. *Communications in Statistics - Theory and Methods*, 7(13):1233–1241, 1978. doi: 10.1080/03610927808827707.

[47] H. M. Markowitz. *Portfolio Selection: Efficient Diversification of Investments*. Wiley, 2 edition, 1991.

[48] J. Matoušek and B. Gärtner. *Understanding and Using Linear Programming*. Springer Berlin Heidelberg New York, 2007.

[49] T. Meinl and M. R. Berthold. Crossover Operators for Multiobjective k-Subset Selection. In *GECCO '09: Proceedings of the 11th Annual conference on Genetic and evolutionary computation*, pages 1809–1810, New York, NY, USA, 2009. ACM. doi: 10.1145/1569901.1570173.

[50] G. Mendel. Versuche über Pflanzenhybriden. *Verhandlungen des naturforschenden Vereines in Brünn*, 4:3–47, 1865.

[51] K. Miettinen. *Introduction to Multiobjective Optimization: Noninteractive Approaches*, volume 5252 of *Lecture Notes in Computer Science*, chapter 1, pages 1–26. Springer, 2008. doi: 10.1007/978-3-540-88908-3.

[52] D. I. Moon and S. S. Chaudhry. An Analysis of Network Location Problems with Distance Constraints. *MANAGEMENT SCIENCE*, 30(3):290–307, March 1984. doi: 10.1287/mnsc.30.3.290.

[53] D. Morent, D. E. Patterson, and M. R. Berthold. Towards context-aware similarity metrics. In *Proceedings of ICMLC'05 (International Conference on Machine Learning and Cybernetics)*, volume 9, pages 5596–5598. IEEE Press, 2005.

[54] S. Nijssen and J. N. Kok. The Gaston Tool for Frequent Subgraph Mining. *Electronic Notes in Theoretical Computer Science*, 127(1):77–87, 2005. doi: 10.1016/j.entcs.2004.12.039, Proceedings of the International Workshop on Graph-Based Tools (GraBaTs 2004).

[55] I. M. Oliver, D. J. Smith, and J. R. C. Holland. A Study of Permutation Crossover Operators on the TSP. In J. J. Grefenstette, editor, *Genetic Algorithms and Their Applications: Proceedings of the Second International Conference*, pages 224–230, Hillsdale, New Jersey, USA, 1987. Lawrence Erlbaum.

[56] M. Padberg. The boolean quadric polytope: Some characteristics, facets and relatives. *Mathematical Programming*, 45(1–3):139–172, August 1989. doi: 10.1007/BF01589101.

[57] K. Park, K. Lee, and S. Park. An extended formulation approach to the edge-weighted maximal clique problem. *European Journal of Operational Research*, 95(3):671–682, December 1996. doi: 10.1016/0377-2217(95)00299-5.

[58] D. E. Patterson, R. D. Cramer, A. M. Ferguson, R. D. Clark, and L. E. Weinberger. Neighborhood Behavior: A Useful Concept for Validation of "Molecular Diversity" Descriptors. *Journal of Medicinal Chemistry*, 39(16):3049–3059, 1996. doi: 10.1021/jm960290n.

[59] D. Pisinger. Upper bounds and exact algorithms for p-dispersion problems. *Computers & Operations Research*, 33(5):1380–1398, May 2006. doi: 10.1016/j.cor.2004.09.033.

[60] M. Rarey and J. S. Dixon. Feature trees: A new molecular similarity measure based on tree matching. *Journal of Computer-Aided Molecular Design*, 12(5):471–490, September 1998. doi: 10.1023/A:1008068904628.

[61] D. S.Hochbaum and D. B. Shmoys. A Best Possible Heuristic for the k-Center Problem. *MATHEMATICS OF OPERATIONS RESEARCH*, 10(2):180–184, May 1985. doi: 10.1287/moor.10.2.180.

[62] Simulations Plus, Inc. ClassPharmer. http://www.simulationsplus.com/Products.aspx?grpID=1&cID=13&pID=12. [Online; accessed 2010-01-26].

[63] A. Sokolov and D. Whitley. Unbiased tournament selection. In *GECCO '05: Proceedings of the 2005 conference on Genetic and evolutionary computation*, pages 1131–1138, New York, NY, USA, 2005. ACM. doi: 10.1145/1068009.1068198.

[64] M. M. Sørensen. New facets and a branch-and-cut algorithm for the weighted clique problem. *European Journal of Operational Research*, 154(1):57–70, April 2004. doi: 10.1016/S0377-2217(02)00852-4.

[65] R. Thiericke. *Modern Methods of Drug Discovery*, chapter High-throughput screening technologies, pages 71–86. Birkhäuser Verlag, Basel, Switzerland, 2003.

[66] J.-F. Truchon and C. I. Bayly. Evaluating Virtual Screening Methods: Good and Bad Metrics for the "Early Recognition" Problem. *Journal of Chemical Information and Modeling*, 47(2):488–508, March 2007. doi: 10.1021/ci600426e.

[67] Y. Wang and C. Maple. A Novel Efficient Algorithm for Determining Maximum Common Subgraphs. In *IV '05: Proceedings of the Ninth International Conference on Information Visualisation (IV'05)*, pages 657–663, Washington, DC, USA, 2005. IEEE Computer Society. doi: 10.1109/IV.2005.11.

[68] M. L. Weitzman. On Diversity. *The Quarterly Journal of Economics*, 107(2):363–405, 1992. doi: 10.2307/2118476.

[69] D. Xin, H. Cheng, X. Yan, and J. Han. Extracting redundancy-aware top-k patterns. In *KDD '06: Proceedings of the 12th ACM SIGKDD international conference on Knowledge discovery and data mining*, pages 444–453, New York, NY, USA, 2006. ACM. doi: 10.1145/1150402.1150452.

[70] X. Yan and J. Han. gSpan: Graph-Based Substructure Pattern Mining. In *Proceedings of the IEEE Intl. Conf. on Data Mining ICDM*, pages 51–58, Piscataway, NJ, USA, 2002. IEEE Press. doi: 10.1109/ICDM.2002.1184038.

[71] E. Zitzler, J. Knowles, and L. Thiele. Quality Assessment of Pareto Set Approximations. In *Multiobjective Optimization - Interactive and Evolutionary Approaches*, volume 5252 of *Lecture Notes in Computer Science*, pages 373–404. Springer, Berlin, Germany, 2008. doi: 10.1007/978-3-540-88908-3_14.

[72] E. Zitzler, M. Laumanns, and L. Thiele. SPEA2: Improving the Strength Pareto Evolutionary Algorithm. Technical Report 103, Swiss Federal Institute of Technology (ETH) Zurich, 2001.

I want morebooks!

Buy your books fast and straightforward online - at one of world's fastest growing online book stores! Environmentally sound due to Print-on-Demand technologies.

Buy your books online at
www.morebooks.shop

Kaufen Sie Ihre Bücher schnell und unkompliziert online – auf einer der am schnellsten wachsenden Buchhandelsplattformen weltweit! Dank Print-On-Demand umwelt- und ressourcenschonend produziert.

Bücher schneller online kaufen
www.morebooks.shop

KS OmniScriptum Publishing
Brivibas gatve 197
LV-1039 Riga, Latvia
Telefax:+371 686 204 55

info@omniscriptum.com
www.omniscriptum.com

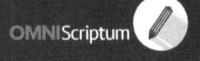

Printed by Books on Demand GmbH, Norderstedt / Germany